Unlocking the Poem

A Guide to Discovering Meaning
through Understanding and Analysis

**MARTIN BELLER &
DONNA CARLSON TANZER**

Sherpa Learning is dedicated to helping high-achieving learners gain access to high-quality, skills-based instruction that is created, reviewed, and tested by teachers. To learn more about Sherpa Learning and our vision, or to learn about some of our upcoming projects, please visit us at **www.sherpalearning.com**.

Publisher/Editor: David Nazarian

Copy-Editor: Christine DeFranco

Proof-Reader: Kristyna Zaharek

Illustrator: Jamari Jackson

Cover Design: David Nazarian

Cover Photograph: Catherine's Alley, Tallinn, Estonia,
© 2016, D. Nazarian

* AP is a registered trademark of the College Board, which was not involved in the production of, and does not endorse, this product.

ISBN 978-1-948641-20-3

Copyright © 2020

Sherpa Learning, LLC.

West Milford, New Jersey

www.sherpalearning.com

All rights reserved. No part of this book may be kept in an information storage or retrieval system, transmitted or reproduced in any form or by any means without prior written permission of the Publisher.

Printed in the United States of America.

10 9 8 7 6 5 4 3 2

TABLE OF CONTENTS

Student Introduction v
Teacher Introduction ix
About the Poets xi

Lesson 1: Sonnet 23
    by William Shakespeare 1

Lesson 2: A Bird came down the Walk
    by Emily Dickinson 8

Lesson 3: The White City
    by Claude McKay 15

Lesson 4: The Armadillo
    by Elizabeth Bishop 23

Lesson 5: Aubade
    by Philip Larkin 33

Student Support
    Lesson 1: Sonnet 23 44
    Lesson 2: A Bird came down the Walk 49
    Lesson 3: The White City 54
    Lesson 4: The Armadillo 61
    Lesson 5: Aubade 68

Table of Contents

The Tool Box
    Introduction to the Tool Box 73
    Section I: Raw Materials 75
    Section II: Seeing and Hearing 77
    Section III: Creating Rhythms 82
    Section IV: Presenting Thoughts 86
    Section V: The Music and Noise of Poetry 92
    Section IV: Types of Poetry 94

About the Authors 97
Acknowledgments 99
Also Available from Sherpa Learning 101

TO THE STUDENT

How do you feel about poetry? Do you enjoy reading poems, or are you afraid you may not understand them? Whatever your attitude toward poetry, this book will help you discover how to read poems more effectively. Starting with your own unique, immediate responses, you will move gradually toward a nuanced and well-supported interpretation. If you follow the process taught in this book, you will find yourself able to read new poems with a sense of discovery, even in testing situations.

Each lesson focuses on a single poem and is organized into five parts:

Read

Each lesson begins by asking you to anticipate the poem by thinking about its title, topic, or anything else you already know about the poem or the poet. Then read the poem using your imagination and feelings. Get to know your way around the poem by reading it more than once. Hear the poem by reading it aloud or listening while someone else reads it.

Respond

After reading the poem, you will write a brief journal response followed by a longer response when you have more ideas about the poem. At this stage of the learning process, the poems belong to you; you can react in any way that seems natural to you.

Inquire

After repeated silent and oral readings of a poem, you will begin to ask questions about it, getting to know the poem much as you get to know the people in your life. Though your own questions are always the best, the lessons provide sample questions for you to discuss and use as models.

Analyze

Only after you have discussed these questions in small groups and with the whole class will you begin to look at poetic elements using the language of poetic analysis. These elements are not simply technical terms to identify but are closely connected to the meanings you have already discovered. With this poetic vocabulary, you will be ready to craft a thoughtful, valid interpretation that is supported by the poem itself and includes your own ideas.

Interpret

Each lesson closes with an essay prompt that you should be well prepared to address. Use your own questions and your understanding of poetic technique to form an interpretation of the poem, and then write an essay to support your interpretation.

Another section of this book is the **Tool Box**, connecting to the "Analyze" section of each lesson. The Tool Box offers even more examples of literary elements, all drawn from the lessons you are studying. You may not need to consult the Tool Box for every lesson, but it provides clarification and additional examples of these poetic techniques.

Welcome to the world of poetry! Enjoy the journey as you discover and develop genuine insights into these powerful classic and contemporary poems.

TO THE TEACHER

It's All About Meaning

The idea behind *Unlocking the Poem* is basic—it's all about the meaning. Serious readers of poetry know intuitively that getting to know a poem is a journey of personal discovery toward a credible, supported interpretation. *Unlocking the Poem* provides a method to help students achieve both personal discovery and valid interpretation. As they study the poems in this book, students will consistently learn and practice the five basic aspects of this approach:

- repeated readings
- making a personal connection with the text
- questioning the text sensitively but insistently
- once insights have been developed, exploring how formal and technical elements affect our experience and interpretation of a poem
- discovering your own meaning by writing about it

Inquiry—Using Students' Questions

At the heart of our method is inquiry—using the students' own reactions to drive discussion and exploration of poems. This method provides a ready-made template for approaching any poem you may choose to teach. While finding their own way into a poem through initial readings and reactions, students will ask questions, formulate thoughts, and share their questions and ideas with others in the class. This is not a rushed "coverage" approach. Students will read and reread a poem several times, an essential step in understanding a poem. They will not only read the poem silently and study its placement on the page, but will also read the poem aloud and listen to its cadences, rhythms, and sound effects.

Flexible Organization

The lessons in *Unlocking the Poem* offer flexibility and adaptability: they can be used in class or as homework and in almost any order. You may use the journal and inquiry activities in the lessons for oral or written responses. Within each lesson, you can move sequentially or selectively through the questions, depending on your students' needs, abilities, and interests. Students can work individually or collectively, preparing creative as well as analytic responses.

The Necessary Tools

Through reading, questioning, and discussing, students will have formed a concept of the "what" of a poem—its basic meaning. The Tool Box will help them unlock the "how" and prepare them to articulate a supportable interpretation of the poem. Central to our approach is the idea that the technical and formal elements derive their importance from their role in leading readers to a deeper understanding of the poem. This is why we urge users of our book to reserve consideration of "poetic devices and techniques"—metaphor, imagery, meter, symbolism, and so forth—until they have developed a sense of the poem's meaning.

Write About It

Each lesson concludes with at least one essay prompt to help teachers and students assess their understanding of the poems. The insights needed to answer these prompts thoroughly and effectively are a product of the repeated readings, the questioning, and the discussions. After students have come to know the process taught in this book, you may occasionally ask them to begin with the prompt to see how well they can write about a poem they have never seen before. In these cases, the lesson can follow the prompt as a means of helping students to understand the strengths and weaknesses in their initial written responses.

Pacing

The lessons in *Unlocking the Poem* offer an abundance of teaching material: generally, more than any class will be able to cover on any single poem. Your judgment as a teacher will always be required to determine how much of each lesson to use with your class. We urge you to remember that although poems are quickly read, they are not quickly understood. They work through suggestion and distillation of meaning, and the intensity and compression of their language often requires extraordinary care and patience to analyze. That said, we offer the following practical suggestions.

1. Decide how you are going to integrate the study of poetry into your course as a whole and how you will be using *Unlocking the Poem* within that context. Poetry makes extraordinary demands on student and teacher alike. Our own experience suggests that the intense study of poetry is best pursued in manageable bits throughout the year, rather than in one enormous gulp; your experience will suggest what works best for you. The format you adopt—comprehensive unit, recurring mini-units, weekly "poetry day," or your own favorite—will help you decide which poems to read and how much time to spend on any given poem or cluster of poems.

2. Review the lesson and suggested responses before assigning a poem from *Unlocking the Poem*. Decide in advance why you are teaching any given poem. If your primary objective

To the Teacher

is simply to provide practice in interpreting poems, you may wish to focus on the questions which lead us to a sound understanding of the poem. If you are focusing more on the connections between form and meaning—if, for example, you are exploring "metaphor" or "imagery"—you may find the devices and techniques in Part 4 of each lesson an important part of your plan. If you use the lesson as the basis for a practice essay, you will want to reserve time for the journaling and other writing prompts.

We hope you—teachers and students alike—will find *Unlocking the Poem* both useful and enjoyable. We leave you on its doorstep, with these final words of support and encouragement: Poems are communications from one person to another. They are not puzzles to be cracked with special tools, nor are they exercises in "using" various poetic devices and techniques. Poetry is, among all the genres of literature, the one best able to move beyond simply depicting feelings to actively expressing them. You can see people feeling love, hate, happiness, and sadness in a story or a play. But to encounter the feelings themselves, you must go to a poem. Poetry is the most immediate, intense, and direct form of literary expression, and we read poems to see in a new way, to feel keenly and freshly. *Unlocking the Poem* was written to make this experience more readily available to all who want it.

Martin Beller
Donna Tanzer

ABOUT THE POETS

William Shakespeare (1564-1616)

William Shakespeare was one of England's most popular writers during his lifetime and has been regarded as its greatest writer since the 18th century. He is most celebrated as the dramatist who created such incomparable plays as *Hamlet*, *Macbeth*, *King Lear*, *Twelfth Night*, and *The Tempest*. But his Sonnets, first published in 1609, also establish him as one of the greatest lyric poets in the English language.

Emily Dickinson (1830-1886)

Emily Dickinson lived a quiet, largely uneventful life, never moving out of her father's home. In her later years, she was a virtual recluse. Although she wrote nearly 1,800 poems, she only permitted a handful of them to be published during her life. Her unconventional poetic style and practice were too idiosyncratic for even her most sympathetic contemporaries. Early editors of her poems imposed consistent meter, rhyme, and punctuation, and it was not until the 1950s that her poems began to appear as she wrote them. By that time, she had become widely recognized as one of the greatest American poets.

Claude McKay (1889-1948)

Jamaican-born Claude McKay was one of many black writers, artists, and musicians who fought for freedom, dignity, and equal rights for African Americans. McKay is regarded as having helped define the spirit of the Harlem Renaissance, and his work influenced the writing of many younger African American poets, including Langston Hughes. Although he immigrated to the United States in 1912 and never returned to his homeland, his writings include novels, autobiographies, and poems of Jamaica in addition to his more well-known social protest poetry.

Elizabeth Bishop (1911-1979)

Essentially orphaned by her father's death and her mother's mental illness, Elizabeth Bishop spent much of her childhood with her grandparents in Nova Scotia, an area she came to idealize in her poems. Her poems are filled with scenic descriptions of her world travels and convey her sense of herself as a traveler without roots. She deplored what she called "confessional" poetry and avoided accounts of her personal life, focusing instead on precise details of the physical world. Although her words often seem whimsically spontaneous, she worked meticulously, often rewriting a single poem for many years. She was the Poet Laureate of the United States from 1949 to 1950.

Philip Larkin (1922-1985)

Philip Larkin was arguably England's greatest poet of the post-WWII period, and is certainly one of its most widely read. His work remains, now more than three decades after his death, both popular among readers and respected by critics and poets. His published output was small, amounting to only four slender volumes during his life. He was celebrated for his refusal to be made a celebrity, spending most of his adult life working as a librarian, a career in which he distinguished himself almost as notably as he did in poetry. Larkin was offered the position of Poet Laureate of England a year before his death, but declined it. Philip Larkin's poetry expresses a pervasive disenchantment with life, but his often-depressing subject matter and disappointed tone are offset by his evident delight in exercising his mastery of the poet's craft.

Lesson 1

Sonnet 23

by William Shakespeare

Read

Anticipate the Poem

What is it like to be so smitten with someone that you are at a loss for words? If you've ever felt that way, try to recapture what it felt like to be almost physically unable to speak. When you feel tongue-tied and can't find the right words, how do you communicate your emotions?

Shakespeare's Sonnet 23 reveals a speaker who faces just such a dilemma.

Read Sonnet 23 straight through, twice. Don't try to stop and figure anything out; rather, just let the poem and its emotions speak to you.

Lesson 1 — Sonnet 23

Sonnet 23

by William Shakespeare

As an unperfect actor on the stage,
Who with his fear is put besides his part,
Or some fierce thing replete*a* with too much rage,
Whose strength's abundance weakens his own heart;
5   So I, for fear of trust, forget to say
The perfect ceremony of love's right*b*,
And in mine own love's strength seem to decay,
O'ercharged*c* with burthen of mine own love's might:
O, let my books*d* be then the eloquence
10 And dumb presagers*e* of my speaking breast,
Who plead for love, and look for recompense*f*,
More than that tongue that more hath more express'd:
   O, learn to read what silent love hath writ:
   To hear with eyes belongs to love's fine wit.

---

a stuffed | *b* that is, 'rite' (ritual), but also 'right' (privilege) | *c* weighed down | *d* "looks" in some editions | *e* messengers | *f* reward, payoff

Respond

Journal

Describe your first impression of Sonnet 23. Write about a line or phrase that interests you, or whatever comes to your mind as you reflect on the speaker's thoughts and feelings.

Read It Aloud

Now read the poem aloud twice, or read it aloud once and listen closely as your teacher or classmate reads it aloud. Think about what the speaker is telling us as you hear the words and ideas. How does the music of the poem's words affect you as you listen? What specific words or phrases strike you as important, beautiful, or particularly hard to understand? Do you hear the deep worry in the speaker's plea to his beloved? Where? What words suggest this worry?

Extended Journal Response

At this point, you are ready to write a fuller response to the poem, exploring the speaker's dilemma and emotions. You might want to connect your own experiences to the speaker's state, such as a time when you felt speechless, or you may want to give advice to the speaker. Don't worry right now about specific phrases and details that are still unclear to you. Rather, respond freely to the speaker and to his plight. You may wish to write your own poem about the challenge of finding words to convey your deepest feelings.

Lesson 1 — Sonnet 23

Inquire

General Inquiries

As you look closely at the specific sections and lines of the poem, again trying to "hear it" as you read, think of questions you can ask. Quickly record three to five general questions about anything at all in the poem. Include things that are unclear to you as well as general ideas you would like to discuss more. Here are two to get you started:

1. What does the speaker compare himself to?
2. What does the speaker say about love and about expressing love?

Inquiries about Words and Phrases

Look more closely at the specifics of the poem as you develop three or four more questions, focusing on specific phrases, images, and lines. Model your questions on these examples:

3. What would an "unperfect actor" be like?
4. What does the speaker mean by "the perfect ceremony of love's right" and "dumb presagers of my speaking breast"?

Inquiries about Attitude and Tone

Now write a few more questions that point to the speaker's purpose or attitude and the poem's overall meaning. Use these to get you started:

5. How is a tongue-tied lover like and unlike an actor with stage fright or a "fierce thing"?
6. What does the speaker want "books" (or "looks") in line 9 to lead to?

7. Since the speaker struggles to express his love in words, what does he want his beloved to do to appreciate the depth of this love?

Directed Inquiries

Here are a few questions that call attention to details you may have overlooked, or be unsure how to bring into an interpretation.

8. How can the words "part" and "books" as well as the phrase "dumb presagers" work together to unify the image of an "unperfect actor"?

9. How is the speaker both like and unlike what we know about Shakespeare himself? How does this affect our sense of who the speaker is?

10. What do the images of excessive strength ("fierce thing," "strength's abundance," "love's strength," "love's might") express and convey about the speaker's feelings?

11. What does it mean to "hear with eyes"? How would the beloved do this, and what would be the desired effect?

Analyze

Let the Speaker Guide You to the Meaning

What can make it hard to understand people is not that they *sometimes* have secrets but that they're *always* mysterious. The sources of their acts and words are hidden within them. We have to rely on their explanations to understand the behaviors and moods they show us. What "mysterious" behavior is the speaker of Sonnet 23 trying to explain? What explanation—what solution to the mystery—does he offer? What does he want the person he is addressing to do, feel, or think?

Lesson 1 — Sonnet 23

Notice and Account for Metrical Variations

The meter of this poem might be labeled iambic pentameter simply because that is the prevailing meter of Shakespeare's sonnets. But there are hardly two consecutive iambs in the first eight lines: only lines 4 and 6 even *begin* with a securely iambic foot. In the last six lines, however, the iambic impulse is dominant. Only "pre SAGE ers of my SPEAK'" in line 10 and the spondees that begin line 12 and end line 14 disturb it. Try to scan the first eight lines of Sonnet 23, and notice the way no single rhythmic pattern ever establishes itself. What is the relationship between the rough, constantly varied metrics of the octave and the smooth regularity of the sestet?

Dig Deeper into Similes

In the octave, the speaker compares himself to two different sorts of people who can't speak: an actor who can't remember his lines because of stage fright; and a person (maybe not even a person, a 'thing') in the grip of a violent passion. Both the similes are introduced in the first quatrain and developed in the second: in both cases, the first two lines are devoted to the first simile ("As an unperfect actor" / "I forget to say") and lines 3-4 are devoted to the second ("[As] some fierce thing" / "[my] strength seems to decay"). How do these two similes help the speaker make his case? How are they more appropriate to the speaker's purpose than, say, attributing his speechlessness to being gagged or having a defective vocal apparatus?

Here's another way to approach the poem's similes: Think about what we know about Shakespeare, and then consider the strangeness of his writing a poem in which he compares himself to a frightened actor and a person rendered inarticulate by overflowing emotions. How does the fact that the poem is written by Shakespeare add a level of irony to the poem?

Interpret

You have now assembled the pieces of a full interpretation of Sonnet 23 and are ready to put the pieces together. Your interpretation should have three elements: a **paraphrase** of each of the poem's three quatrains and the couplet; an **explication** of what the poem's statements mean to the speaker—what he wants the recipient to know, to think, to feel, and to do; and an **evaluation** of the speaker's success in explaining his behavior.

Write About It

Write an essay in which you analyze the speaker in Shakespeare's Sonnet 23. Discuss the mystery of the speaker's role, his intention, and his desires. Include in your essay how such literary devices as similes, irony, and metrical variation work to communicate the speaker's dilemma.

Lesson 2

A Bird came down the Walk

by Emily Dickinson

Read

Anticipate the Poem

The title of a poem will often provide enough information or suggestions to permit us to anticipate much about its content. It may offer clues to the poem's subject, ideas, or tone. Emily Dickinson didn't give her poems titles so their first lines have traditionally identified them. In a way, this is appropriate, since many of her first lines are so powerful and direct that they might almost be said to contain the essence of the whole poem.

Consider the first line of the poem, "A Bird came down the Walk." What information can you derive just from this single line? Spend a few minutes with it. Hold it up to the light and look at it from several angles. Then write in your poetry journal whatever it suggests to you about the poem that will grow out of it.

"A Bird came down the Walk" is a brief poem. It contains twenty short lines and just over 100 words. Read it through a few times just to fix the action in your mind. You will immediately see that the first twelve lines report on what anybody might observe while watching a bird. But then the poem flies off in an unexpected direction and becomes harder to follow.

Unlocking the Poem

A Bird came down the Walk

by Emily Dickinson

A Bird came down the Walk—
He did not know I saw—
He bit an Angleworm in halves
And ate the fellow, raw,

5   And then he drank a Dew
From a convenient Grass—
And then hopped sidewise to the Wall
To let a Beetle pass—

He glanced with rapid eyes
10   That hurried all around—
They looked like frightened Beads, I thought—
He stirred his Velvet Head

Like one in danger, Cautious,
I offered him a Crumb
15   And he unrolled his feathers
And rowed him softer home—

Than Oars divide the Ocean,
Too silver for a seam—
Or Butterflies off Banks of Noon
20   Leap, plashless as they swim.

Lesson 2 — A Bird came down the Walk

Respond

Journal

Even though the first twelve lines report on typical bird behavior, Dickinson sometimes asks words to do unfamiliar things. Make a note of anything unusual or hard to understand about the scene she describes.

Then write briefly about what it is like to watch an animal that doesn't know you are observing it. We're not really thinking about bugs here, but if bugs are all you've ever watched, think of bugs. A remembered experience at a Petting Zoo will do, too. Think about your awareness of your own body in such a situation, the position and placement of yourself and the animal, your feelings and thoughts. Was it like watching a nature program? Or was it more like momentarily finding yourself a part of nature?

Read It Aloud

Most poems reveal some unsuspected features when you read them aloud. But few reveal as much as dramatically as "A Bird came down the Walk." Listen to the poem as it is read. Listen to yourself as you read it aloud two or three times. You will probably notice or hear the difference in sound between the first 11 lines and the last 9. Record some initial impressions of the poem in your journal.

Extended Journal Response

Describe in detail the action during the first part of the poem—the first 11 or 12 lines. What is happening during the second part of the poem—the last 8 or 9 lines? How does the speaker seem to feel during the first part of the poem? During the second part? Try to answer these questions using details from the poem to support your answers.

Unlocking the Poem

Inquire

General Inquiries

Quickly write three to five general questions of your own about anything in the poem—a line, a word, or a concept. Here are three examples to help you get started:

1. How does the poem change between the first part and the second part?
2. What's up with the unusual capitalization and all those dashes?
3. Who is the main character in the story, the bird or the speaker?

Inquiries about Words and Phrases

Now ask four or five more questions, looking even more closely at words, images, and lines of the poem.

4. Why does the bird bite an angleworm "in halves"—why not "in half"?
5. Why does the bird drink "a Dew" from "a ... Grass" rather than "some Dew" from "the Grass"?
6. Why does the speaker point out that the bird ate the worm "raw"? Was she expecting the bird to sprinkle it over some pizza and pop it in the oven?

Inquiries about Attitude and Tone

Now ask four or five questions about the speaker's attitude and the way the ideas are organized. Use these questions to get started:

7. Why does the poem's tone change between the first and second parts of the poem? (Lines 1-12 and lines 13-20.)

Lesson 2 — A Bird came down the Walk

8. Is there any difference between the way the speaker sees the bird and the way the bird sees itself?

Directed Inquiries

Here are a few more specific and pointed questions. Let these questions (and any more you might have) direct you toward a fuller interpretation of the poem.

9. Why is the speaker observing the bird so closely? What does the speaker want from the bird?
10. If the poem tells a story, what is the conflict?
11. In what sense is the bird in this poem a "poetry bird"? In what sense is it a real bird?
12. Refer back to question 7, above. Does the change in tone correspond to a change in feeling? Do the speaker's feelings about the bird change between the poem's two parts?
13. Who is "like one in danger, cautious"?
14. How many different elements or aspects of nature has Dickinson managed to include in this poem?

Analyze

Fill in the Ellipses

One of the ways poets say a lot in a few words is through ellipsis—leaving out words that are necessary to the grammar or the sense. Ellipsis is an element that often makes poetry challenging to read and understand, but it also makes it fun. Find places in the poem where something happens, but we're not told what it is. Locate places where a traditional storyteller would give us some information that the poet leaves out.

Evaluate Imagery

A poem can bring a scene to vivid life with a few details. The first part of "A Bird came down the Walk" is rich with images of bird behavior. Look closely again at the first twelve lines, and try to figure out how Dickinson's choice of details and her manner of presenting them enable us to watch the bird with the speaker. Why did Dickinson choose these particular details? How does she seem to feel, or expect us to feel, about the bird? How does she communicate these feelings to us?

Identify Metonymy and Unpack Similes and Metaphors

There is only one simile in the poem, in line 11, where the bird's eyes are likened to "frightened beads." And there is only one instance that might be mistaken for a metaphor in the first part of the poem: "He glanced with *rapid* eyes / That *hurried all around*" (lines 9–10). It isn't the bird's eyes that are rapid and hurrying, but its "glances." That means it is not truly a metaphor. The bird's eyes are not being compared to something that is rapid and hurries. It's simply that the rapidity and hurry of the bird's darting glance is being attributed to its eyes. That's actually *metonymy*, another variety of figurative language.

But the poem ends in a thicket of metaphors so dense that it is difficult to disentangle one from another. Your job is to try to determine what is being compared to what in the last six lines, and how the things being compared are alike. When you have done that, speculate as to why Dickinson chose these metaphors. How do they affect our interpretation of the poem?

Interpret

You have now examined this poem closely and exposed its inescapably strange heart. What appears at first to be just an observation of an insignificant moment—a little nature poem

Lesson 2 — A Bird came down the Walk

about an adorable birdie—becomes an enraptured encounter with mysterious powers. Write a brief explication in which you attempt to do justice to both aspects of the poem.

Write About It

From one perspective, "A Bird came down the Walk" takes its place in a tradition of nature poetry in which the speaker has a momentary interaction with nature and then responds to the moment. In a well-organized essay, describe the way such elements as imagery, characterization, and structure combine to bring to life speaker's experience and her response.

Lesson 3

The White City
by Claude McKay

Read

Anticipate the Poem

A poem's title often provides important clues to its content and should not be overlooked. Before you read Claude McKay's poem, think about the title "The White City" for a moment. What kind of city do you visualize? What makes it white? Is it a real or imaginary city? A little background on Claude McKay will provide some clues, but that will come later. For now, just close your eyes and gaze upon that white city.

Read the poem once, silently. Then read it again, this time aloud, and think about how the poem reflects the title.

Lesson 3 — The White City

The White City
by Claude McKay

I will not toy with it nor bend an inch.
Deep in the secret chambers of my heart
I muse my life-long hate, and without flinch
I bear it nobly as I live my part.
My being would be a skeleton, a shell,
If this dark Passion that fills my every mood,
And makes my heaven in the white world's hell,
Did not forever feed me vital blood.
I see the mighty city through a mist—
The strident trains that speed the goaded mass,
The poles and spires and towers vapor-kissed,
The fortressed port through which the great
    ships pass,
The tides, the wharves, the dens I contemplate,
Are sweet like wanton loves because I hate.

Respond

Recall what the poem's title originally meant to you. How does this correspond to your perception of the poem now? Would it have helped for you to know that Claude McKay was a Jamaican-born black man who lived most of his adult life in New York City? McKay was also an early member of the Harlem Renaissance movement who inspired such prominent writers as Langston Hughes, Zora Neale Hurston, and James Weldon Johnson. "The White City" first appeared in McKay's *Harlem Shadows*, published in 1922. What do the title and the poem say to you now? Knowledge of a poet's background is not essential to our grasp of a poem's meaning, but it can deepen our understanding.

Journal

Write down what you originally thought the title meant. In a paragraph or two, contrast your early thoughts with how you now view McKay's white city. How does McKay's speaker feel about this city? What city do you think this might be? Why? What does it look like in your mind?

Read It Aloud

Working with a partner, practice reading the poem aloud. Pay close attention to the punctuation. Don't stop or pause at the ends of unpunctuated lines, but pause only for the time it takes your eye to move from one line to the next. Decide with your partner what tone of voice will work best. What words or phrases will you emphasize? What different units of thought do you see in the poem?

Extended Journal Response

Choose two or three phrases or lines that you like best or that stand out in some way for you. You might also choose a phrase or

Lesson 3 — The White City

line that you think best reflects the meaning of the entire poem or simply one that sounds appealing or interesting. What makes these lines and phrases stand out for you? What do they say, and how do they say it? Accompany your writing with a rough sketch if you like—especially if you have chosen words or phrases that lend themselves to a drawing.

Inquire

General Inquiries

You have probably noticed that this poem reflects intense emotion, predominantly hate. Write down three to five questions about the expression of hate or anything at all in the poem, modeling your questions on these examples:

1. How does the speaker feel about his own hatred?
2. Toward what is the speaker's hate directed? How long has he felt it?
3. What are some of the things he sees when he looks at the city?

Inquiries about Words and Phrases

Look more closely now at the speaker's language—specifically at words that describe either his emotions or the city. Ask four or five more questions about these word choices. Here are three to get you started:

4. Why does the speaker "muse" his hate?
5. What does he mean by "this dark Passion"? Why "dark"? Why is "Passion" capitalized?
6. What are "wanton loves," and why are they sweet?

Unlocking the Poem

Inquiries about Attitude and Tone

Now consider the speaker and his attitude. Write four or five more questions about the speaker and why he feels as he does. First, answer the questions below, and then use them as examples:

7. Why does the speaker think his hatred is good for him?
8. In addition to hate, what emotions does this poem convey?
9. Why doesn't the speaker mention the white city until nine lines into the poem?

Directed Inquiries

The best questions are often those you learn to ask by yourself. If you have read the poem closely, you may have already asked some of the following questions. They are offered to add depth and nuance to your discussion of the poem.

10. What is "it" in the first line of the poem?
11. Why does the speaker say that his passion "makes my heaven in the white world's hell"? Doesn't this seem to be the opposite of what is expected? Why is he celebrating something he also abhors?
12. Where does the speaker seem to be in relation to the city? Why does this matter?
13. Is the description of the "mighty city" a positive or negative portrayal, or both? In what ways?

Lesson 3 — The White City

Analyze

Contemplate the Setting and Its Purpose

Determining the setting is not a challenge here: the title clearly tells us it is "the white city," which McKay also calls "the mighty city" in line 9. From this description and considering McKay's own life, most critics and readers agree that it is New York City.

In what sense does McKay see New York City of the early 1920's as "white" and "mighty"? Is his poem an indictment of ordinary white people in general, or does he vent his hatred toward more systemic racism? Explain.

There are two significant purposes of setting, or scene, in poetry: the poet may set the scene where something important is enacted, or he or she may describe a place and reflect on the feelings connected with it.

What is the purpose of the setting in "The White City"? Since only the last six lines specifically describe the setting, how can we say that the entire poem imparts setting meaningfully? What references to setting occur in the first eight lines?

Connect Sonnet Form to Meaning

Look closely at the form of "The White City," and observe the transitions in the speaker's thoughts. Note that it is a Shakespearean sonnet, with three quatrains and a couplet.

How do the transitions in the speaker's thoughts follow the structure, meter, and rhyme scheme of a Shakespearean sonnet? How are the third quatrain and couplet connected grammatically so that these lines almost appear to be a sestet, as in a Petrarchan sonnet? What does this close connection suggest?

Why is the sonnet form, with its elevated diction and strict formal requirements, well suited to this speaker's emotional expression? Sonnets are traditionally about love. In what sense is this a "love poem"? In what sense is it not a love poem?

Unlocking the Poem

Examine Speaker and Tone

Clearly, the speaker is expressing hate. But take a closer look at just how he expresses hate, at the nuanced emotions that complicate his hate. Think about the social mechanism underlying the city he describes and how this social structure leads directly to the poem's emotional tone. How does the tone embrace the polar opposites of hate and love? Where else do we see antithesis in the speaker's words and tone? How does he create order, restraint, and even beauty from frustration and resentment?

Interpret

Return to your partners or small groups and read the poem yet again—aloud. Attempt to express the mixed emotions of resentment, frustration, hate, pride, longing, and love that the speaker conveys in this poem. You should be able at this point to interpret the poem as a whole. Summarize briefly how the speaker introduces us to his bitter hatred and then leads us to see how this hate feeds his soul and keeps him alive. Discuss his love-hate relationship with the city he can only see as a disenfranchised outsider looking in through the veil of whiteness.

Write About It

Write a unified essay in which you examine the speaker's complex relationship with the city setting. Include in your analysis a discussion of such literary elements as diction, tone, and structure.

Lesson 3 — The White City

Lesson 4

The Armadillo

by Elizabeth Bishop

Read

Anticipate the Poem

Although this poem is called "The Armadillo," its title creature doesn't show up until the eighth stanza. As you read the poem, ask yourself why this fellow is important enough to earn the title spot despite his late entrance.

The opening stanzas, rather, take us to a Brazilian "Festa Junina" ("June festival," in this case for St. John's Day) where "illegal fire balloons" light up the skies. The custom of releasing these balloons persists in Brazil and other places even though it is an environmental crime punishable with fines and imprisonment. Elizabeth Bishop's poem revels in the beauty and excitement of the released balloons while also warning of their danger.

Elizabeth Bishop is noted for her restraint, even in poems that evoke an emotional response. Keeping this restraint in mind will work in your favor as you read "The Armadillo" silently. Look for a shift as we move from the speaker's description of the fire balloons rising into the sky to her later focus on affected animals and their habitats. What then happens—what kind of jolt does the closing stanza deliver? How do these changes affect what you see in your mind as you read?

Lesson 4 — The Armadillo

The Armadillo
by Elizabeth Bishop

This is the time of year
when almost every night
the frail, illegal fire balloons appear.
Climbing the mountain height,

rising toward a saint
still honored in these parts,
the paper chambers flush and fill with light
that comes and goes, like hearts.

Once up against the sky it's hard
to tell them from the stars—
planets, that is—the tinted ones:
Venus going down, or Mars,

or the pale green one. With a wind,
they flare and falter, wobble and toss;
but if it's still they steer between
the kite sticks of the Southern Cross,

receding, dwindling, solemnly
and steadily forsaking us,
or, in the downdraft from a peak,
suddenly turning dangerous.

Unlocking the Poem

Last night another big one fell.
It splattered like an egg of fire
against the cliff behind the house.
The flame ran down. We saw the pair

of owls who nest there flying up
and up, their whirling black-and-white
stained bright pink underneath, until
they shrieked up out of sight.

The ancient owls' nest must have burned.
Hastily, all alone,
a glistening armadillo left the scene,
rose-flecked, head down, tail down,

and then a baby rabbit jumped out,
short-eared, to our surprise.
So soft!—a handful of intangible ash
with fixed, ignited eyes.

Too pretty, dreamlike mimicry!
O falling fire and piercing cry
and panic, and a weak mailed fist
clenched ignorant against the sky!

Respond

Journal

You have just learned about the custom of celebrating with fire balloons. How does this celebration sound like the Fourth of July? How is it different? What are your first thoughts about this practice?

Read It Aloud

When you look at this poem on the page, you will likely notice its four-line stanzas (quatrains). Do not let these stanzaic divisions dictate your reading; rather, as you read aloud, pay attention to punctuation, pausing slightly for commas and slightly more for dashes. Let your voice come to a complete stop for periods whether they are in the middle of a line or at the end. Applying a restrained, objective tone to your oral reading will serve this poem best until the closing stanza, where the two exclamation points call for a more excitable vocal tone.

As you read the poem aloud, or listen to it being read, focus on the word choices that make the fire balloons an exciting and beautiful spectacle as well as those that make you understand the impact they have on nature and wildlife. Trace the events of the poem as the speaker takes you from the ethereal beauty of the balloons rising amidst the planets through the speaker's distanced awareness of the danger and then to the final exclamations.

Extended Journal Response

Find two or three phrases in the poem that suggest the beauty and thrill of the fire balloons ascending into the sky and a few more that illustrate the danger to nature and wildlife. In a journal entry, explore how these phrases suggest the speaker's attitude toward this celebration. What does she think about the illegal practice of releasing fire balloons? Alternatively, imagine that you are a young child witnessing one of these festivals. Write firsthand about your response to the sight of the balloons or the discovery of the animals—or both.

Inquire

General Inquiries

Reread "The Armadillo." Then ask yourself three or four questions about anything at all that comes to mind regarding the poem. Here are a few examples:

1. Why is this poem called "The Armadillo" instead of something like "The Fire Balloons" or even "Animals in Danger"?
2. What is the point of all the references to planets and stars?
3. When do the fire balloons turn dangerous? Who is most vulnerable to their hazards?
4. How does the closing stanza markedly change the poem's mood and impact?

Inquiries about Words and Phrases

Keep going. Start making your questions more specific as you zero in on specific words and phrases. Ask yourself what they mean, like this:

5. What makes the illegal fire balloons "frail"? Can you find other word choices that tie in with this idea of frailty? What other words and phrases suggest traits or qualities of the balloons?
6. Notice that the balloons are "rising toward a saint / still honored in these parts"? Where is the saint—why "rising"? What does "still honored" suggest about

the festivities? Is there a religious element to the ceremonies? If you think so, why and how? If not, explain.

7. Why do the balloons "flush and fill with light / that comes and goes"?

8. Why are the owls and armadillo both described in pink hues (the owls are "stained pink underneath" and the armadillo is "rose-flecked")?

9. What is a "mailed fist"? How effective is this mailed fist against the destructive impact of the fire?

Inquiries about Attitude and Tone

Now let your questions move into an essential poetic element—the speaker and her tone. Where is she going with this poem?

10. How does the speaker react to the sight of the ascending balloons?

11. How does the speaker react as she first notices the owls, the armadillo, and the rabbit? Is she upset about what she sees? If so, to what extent?

12. How does the final stanza differ from the rest of the poem? List all the specific differences you see between the first eight stanzas and the ninth. How do these changes help drive home the poem's meaning?

Directed Inquiries

Here are a few more specific and pointed questions, ideas that may have crossed your mind as you thought about the poem as a whole, its words and phrases, and its tone. Let these questions (and any more you might have) direct you toward a fuller interpretation of the poem—possibly an application that moves us from the Brazilian festival to our humanity and our world.

Unlocking the Poem

13. Festa Junina remains hugely popular in Brazil to celebrate the end of the summer harvest. St. John's Day, June 24, is just one piece of the overall festival. What is ironic about the saint's day aspect of the festivities as described here?

14. What do the balloons remind you of as they "flush and fill with light / that comes and goes like hearts"? Why are they "steadily forsaking us" a few stanzas later? What might we associate with them at these junctures?

15. How does the condition caused by "the downdraft from a peak" quickly become not just a potential hazard but a definite and tangible outcome? When are we first aware that the balloons have caused real damage?

16. When the speaker tells us of the destruction of the owls' habitat, she quickly interrupts herself to tell us of the armadillo scurrying away and then the baby rabbit jumping out, even cutting off the description of the rabbit's reaction to note his short ears. Why do you think she interrupts herself so much? How do these interruptions affect you as you process and respond to the scene?

17. How does the speaker feel about the scene she is describing? Does her reaction change at all? If so, when and how? Cite words and images to show how the speaker reacts to what she describes.

18. Of the animal victims described—the owls, the armadillo, the rabbit—which comes closest to wearing "mail" (armor)? Thus, whose perspective do we have in the final stanza? Is there an actual change in the speaker here? If so, what is it?

19. Forces that are both beautiful and dangerous—like the balloons—exist both within us and outside of us. Cite several examples of such beautiful yet dangerous things,

and explain their contradictory attractions. Apply this same contradiction to the poem as you try to extend the poem's ideas beyond the literal narrative.

Analyze

Recognize Shifts in the Speaker's Tone.

The questions above and those you came up with should help you to trace the speaker's tone throughout the poem. What does she feel as she watches the balloons rise to take their place in the planetary sky? What specific words signify the upward trajectory of the balloons? When does the speaker first note their danger—and with what words? What is the effect of the change from "up" and away ("receding, dwindling") to "down" ("downward draft")? Look closely—line by line—at the speaker's tone and try to describe it as she takes us through each of these changes. (Hint: Look back at the "Read It Aloud" section to help you discern tone.)

When do we see a complete and dramatic change in tone? How do diction, punctuation, and form create this change? How is the speaker's perspective different? Does this seem like the same speaker who has stayed at arm's length to relate the "storyline" of the poem—the releasing of the balloons, their ascent, the wind draft that causes them to "splatter," and the resulting impact on owls, armadillo, and rabbit? What happens to our perspective as we move into this final stanza?

Examine Both Figurative and Concrete Imagery

Consider the impact of both figurative and concrete images throughout "The Armadillo." Bishop gives us two striking and highly visual similes for the balloons. What quality do they convey as they "flush and fill with light / …like hearts"? When you learn that one "splattered like an egg of fire," can you see a metaphor inside the simile? What do words like "splattered" and "egg" make you think of? Later, how does Bishop's rabbit metaphor, "a handful of intangible ash," both describe and foreshadow?

Now go on to look at the concrete imagery: the owls' "whirling black-and-white /stained pink underneath." What is black and white, and what is that pink stain? Why is the "glistening armadillo" also "rose-flecked"? What are we actually visualizing seeing that is "pink" or "rose"? How do these images pull us, as readers, into the aftermath of the celebration?

Interpret

Now you are ready to bring several ideas about "The Armadillo" together into a cohesive interpretation of the poem. In your unified interpretive statement, show how the speaker offers two almost irreconcilable views of the festive balloons. Your task here is to show how Bishop's tone and imagery lead us to realize and even experience what those celebratory balloons do. How does "dreamlike mimicry" bring the poem full circle to its conclusion? How does the startling last stanza tie everything together? If it leaves you both thinking and feeling, try to articulate both what it makes you think about and how it makes you feel. Try, too, not to stop with this literal interpretation. Besides the impact of fire balloons on wildlife, what else might this poem suggest in a universal sense? What might it say about humans?

Write About It

In "The Armadillo," Elizabeth Bishop juxtaposes the beauty and hazards of the fire balloons released during a Brazilian festival. Analyze the poem in a thoughtful essay, considering what this juxtaposition suggests about both wildlife and human nature. In your essay, pay close attention to such literary elements as imagery, figurative language, and tone.

Lesson 4 — The Armadillo

Lesson 5

Aubade

by Philip Larkin

Read

Anticipate the Poem

If you don't already know what the word means, look up the definition and history of "aubade." What is an "aubade"? What can we expect from one? Can you think of any modern songs that are, or are like, aubades?

"Aubade" is a long and thought-crammed poem that clearly will require more than one reading just to yield its basic sense—its paraphraseable content. Reread it several times to become familiar with its shape, its tone, and the way it treats its subject. It is quickly apparent that the poem has something to do with "unresting death," and it should gradually become evident that the poem is a meditation on the idea that we know we will die, and that we have feelings about this.

Lesson 5 — Aubade

Aubade

by Philip Larkin

I work all day, and get half-drunk at night.
Waking at four to soundless dark, I stare.
In time the curtain-edges will grow light.
Till then I see what's really always there:
Unresting death, a whole day nearer now,
Making all thought impossible but how
And where and when I shall myself die.
Arid interrogation: yet the dread
Of dying, and being dead,
Flashes afresh to hold and horrify.

The mind blanks at the glare. Not in remorse
—The good not done, the love not given, time
Torn off unused—nor wretchedly because
An only life can take so long to climb
Clear of its wrong beginnings, and may never;
But at the total emptiness for ever,
The sure extinction that we travel to
And shall be lost in always. Not to be here,
Not to be anywhere,
And soon; nothing more terrible, nothing more true.

This is a special way of being afraid
No trick dispels. Religion used to try,
That vast moth-eaten musical brocade
Created to pretend we never die,
And specious stuff that says No rational being
Can fear a thing it will not feel, not seeing
That this is what we fear—no sight, no sound,
No touch or taste or smell, nothing to think with,
Nothing to love or link with,
The anaesthetic from which none come round.

And so it stays just on the edge of vision,
A small unfocused blur, a standing chill
That slows each impulse down to indecision.
Most things may never happen: this one will,
And realisation of it rages out
In furnace-fear when we are caught without
People or drink. Courage is no good:
It means not scaring others. Being brave
Lets no one off the grave.
Death is no different whined at than withstood.

Slowly light strengthens, and the room takes shape.
It stands plain as a wardrobe, what we know,
Have always known, know that we can't escape,
Yet can't accept. One side will have to go.
Meanwhile telephones crouch, getting ready to ring
In locked-up offices, and all the uncaring
Intricate rented world begins to rouse.
The sky is white as clay, with no sun.
Work has to be done.
Postmen like doctors go from house to house.

Respond

Journal

If it's not too personal, what are your own ideas about death—what do you think it will be like to die or to be dead? How do you feel about the fact that you will die? If that's something you'd prefer not to think about right now, take a step back to ask what it is about death that makes us so unwilling to think about it.

Read It Aloud

The poem is full of sounds, though it doesn't depend on sound

Lesson 5 — Aubade

for its impact. The effects are irregular and playful, including the rhyme scheme, which is amazingly complicated when you look at it carefully. "Aubade" asks only to be read intelligently—that is, as the thoughts of an intelligent person. The sense of the sentences as sentences will provide all of the basic rhythmic energy. Many lines are fully and comfortably end-stopped—the first four lines, for example—but this is only because the poet, Philip Larkin, has made those clauses end at line-ends. When the sentences run over the ends of the lines (as at lines 6-7, 8-9, 12-13-14-15, 17-18, and many others), read through the line-break with as little hesitation or pause as your eye-skip will permit.

Extended Journal Response

The poem considers several different aspects of death: did any of them particularly interest or surprise you? Is each verse about a different aspect of the fear of death? Use this writing opportunity to look at each verse as a separate unit of meaning. Try to establish what each verse says and what we're meant to think about its statements.

Inquire

General Inquiries

Begin by asking some questions about the poem as a whole that occur to you or persist after the first few readings. Here are a few examples:

1. Why is this poem called "Aubade"? Given what we know about aubades, how is this an aubade?
2. Is it true that there is "nothing more terrible" than "not to be here"? Is it true that there is "nothing more true"? If not, why might someone think or say these things?

3. Why does this have to be happening at four in the morning?
4. Do you have any feelings about or attitudes toward the speaker? Do you think Larkin meant for us to feel this way?

Inquiries about Words and Phrases

Continue with questions about particular words and phrases.

5. What does "one side will have to go" mean? What are the "sides"? Why will one "have to go"?
6. What is the effect of the speaker characterizing religion as a "moth-eaten musical brocade"? What else is he saying about religion? How does this fit with the rest of what he's saying in the poem?
7. What is the "specious stuff" he mentions? Who says this "specious stuff"?
8. What is "furnace-fear"?
9. Is there any significance to the repetition of "work" in the poem's first and next-to-last line?

Questions about Attitude and Tone

Now you can start formulating an interpretation by asking questions about attitude and tone.

10. How does the speaker feel about death?
11. What are the aspects of knowing he will die that he takes up in the successive verses? What makes each of them terrible, according to the speaker?
12. Is there any resolution in the poem—that is, does anything change or happen in the course of the poem, or is "the dread / of dying and being dead" all it is about?

When we get to the end, have we or the speaker arrived anywhere new, or have we just been circling that single idea?

Analyze

Pay Careful Attention to Speaker and Point of View

The speaker wants us to know who he is: he gives us a couple of facts about himself in line 1, and the way he gives them also tells us something about him. (For example, that he doesn't care much what we think of him—he's not trying to impress us—and that in fact, he doesn't have a particularly impressive life.) But he doesn't give us any further information about himself after that first line, and he doesn't use the word "I" after line 4, or talk about himself at all after line 7. Try to trace the connection between the speaker's attitudes and attributes and the poem's statements about death: is the 'special way of being afraid' something this speaker is especially subject to, or is it a more universal fear?

Make Metaphors Pay their Way

Another striking feature of "Aubade" is its metaphors. Several of them call attention to themselves for their cleverness or virtuosity—"time torn off unused," religion as a "vast, moth-eaten musical brocade," death as "The anaesthetic from which none comes round," and the dazzling cluster of metaphors and similes in the final lines: "telephones crouch . . . the uncaring, intricate, rented world . . . Postmen like doctors . . ." These metaphors are spectacular, but what do they have to do with night sweats? Figurative language usually does more than merely adorn lines of poetry—the metaphors and similes point to meanings beyond themselves. How do these do so?

Don't Take Rhyme for Granted

"Aubade" is almost an encyclopedia entry on the potential of rhyme. There are many different kinds of rhyme in the poem and several rhyme schemes within each verse. There's subtractive rhyme (dread / dead); slant-rhyme (remorse / because); eye rhyme (here / anywhere); identical, both masculine (out / without) and feminine (think with / link with); assonance (rouse / house), internal (the remarkable sequence from the first verse, "day / waking / day / making"); a type of rhyme we don't yet have a name for (ring / uncaring); and even a few "perfect" or "true" rhymes (night / light, now / how, and of course dread / dead). The pattern of rhymes within the ten-line stanzas is similarly wide-ranging, beginning with an alternate rhyming quatrain (ABAB), pausing for a couplet (CC), and culminating in what is technically called an 'enclosing' quatrain' (DEED). See if you can suggest some connection or relationship between these elaborations of rhyme and the poem's essential meaning.

Interpret

"Aubade" presents the reader with a series of challenges: to understand the poem's statements on a sentence-by-sentence basis; to reconcile the down-to-earth working person we encounter in the first verse with the philosophically and poetically sophisticated voice we hear in the subsequent verses; and to articulate the poem's final position or ultimate statement—if there is one. How can our scattered observations about the poem's technique and meaning, its sound and sense, be brought together in a single statement that does justice to all these components?

Write About It

In his poem "Aubade," Philip Larkin explores our human

preoccupation with death. In a thoughtful and well-organized essay, show how Larkin applies such poetic elements as rhyme, figurative language, and stanza form to an examination of our ideas and feelings about death.

STUDENT SUPPORT

The philosophy underlying *Unlocking the Poem* is simple: it's all about the meaning. Getting to know a poem is a journey of personal discovery toward a credible, supported interpretation. The lessons in *Unlocking the Poem* provide a method to help you achieve both personal discovery and valid interpretation. As you study poems in this series, you will consistently learn and practice four basic aspects of this approach. The first three elements of this approach are repeated readings, making a personal connection with the text, and questioning the text sensitively but insistently. The fourth element, undertaken only after the development of insight, is the linking of formal and technical elements to a sound interpretation.

We hope these lessons will nurture your pleasure in encountering poems while also helping you to develop sound interpretations. Our plan is for you to learn poetry through poems, not through literary elements or chronology, to experience poems as intimate communications from one person to another. At the same time, you will be analyzing the ways poetic technique—the technical resources poets have at their disposal—can be conduits to your understanding of the ideas and emotions poems embody.

Inquiry—Using Your Questions

At the heart of our method is inquiry—using your own questions to drive discussion and exploration of poems. This method will be effective with any poem. While finding your own way into a poem through initial readings and reactions, you will ask questions, formulate thoughts, and share their questions and ideas with others in the class. This is not a rushed "coverage" approach. We believe that reading a poem several times is the path to understanding it: silent reading to develop a familiarity with each poem's words and statements; reading aloud to listen to its cadences, rhythms, and sound effects.

There is almost no limit to the questions you can ask. You can look at every word in a poem, recognizing and honoring the poet's careful diction. With the help of the sample questions—a dozen or more in each lesson—you can find your way from basic questions about the meaning of individual words and the content of poetic statements to more open-ended and thought-provoking questions that lead to in-depth insights into meaning and intention.

The Tool Box

After you have become familiar with a poem, formulated questions and sought answers, we ask you to move to the next step: the Tool Box. We cannot overstate the importance of postponing discussion of the formal elements of poetry until after you have developed a sense of meaning. Little is gained if you merely hunt for poetic devices. Discovering meaning will give you ownership and helps you to develop an interpretation of the poem as a whole. Through reading, questioning, and discussing, you will have formed a concept of the "what" of a poem—its basic meaning. The Tool Box will help you unlock the "how" and prepare you to articulate a supportable interpretation of the poem.

Student Essays

Each lesson concludes with an essay prompt to help you show your understanding of the poem. The insights needed to answer these prompts thoroughly and effectively are a product of the repeated readings, the questioning, and the discussions. You also have the option of beginning with the prompt to see how well you can write about a poem you have never seen before. In these cases, you can use the lesson to help you identify the strengths and weaknesses in your initial written responses.

The process of getting inside a poem should be a leisurely one. The questions you ask and answer, the meanings you find, and the connections you make will help you arrive at deeper insights. You will find yourself becoming a stronger reader and better thinker. Most important, as you read and listen to the eloquent voices of great poets, you may be encouraged to reflect more deeply on what it means to be human.

Lesson 1

Sonnet 23
by William Shakespeare

Read

Anticipate: The poem throws a lot of words, images, and similes at us, but there are two surprisingly explicit phrases that may direct us toward the poem's meaning: "Who plead for love and look for recompense," and "learn to read." The first tells us what the speaker wants, and the second tells the recipient how to make this happen.

Respond

Read It Aloud: This poem both welcomes and rewards intelligent reading. All that is required is a moderately slow and undramatic reading of the words. Slow reading will allow the luxuriant vowels to breathe, and the intricacy of thought to become apparent. Try to let the conversational rhythms of lines 1-8 to determine which syllables to emphasize. For example, in line 7 you might emphasize four consecutive syllables ("own love's strength seem") The last six lines fall comfortably into a pretty smooth iambic regularity.

Inquire

General Inquiries

1. The speaker makes two comparisons. He is like "an unperfect actor ... [or] some fierce thing."

2. The speaker claims that "books" though they don't speak aloud, can be as expressive of love and as

deserving of being loved in return as the most passionate speaker.

Inquiries about Words and Phrases

3. What would an "unperfect" actor be like?—one who either can't remember his or her lines ("his part") or who is unhinged by stage fright ("his fear").

4. This question asks you to interpret an ambiguous phrase. It may be too early to decide what the phrase does mean but not to begin thinking about what it might mean. Other phrases that don't yield immediate sense are found in lines 3, 4, 5, 6, 7, and 12.

Inquiries about Attitude and Tone

5. Both the tongue-tied lover and the "unperfect actor" are silent or inarticulate when they should be fluent and both may feel they have forever lost something they desperately want. The "fierce thing," because we don't know just what it is, does not yield such an abundance of apt points of comparison. At bottom, both are prevented from speaking not by having nothing to say but by having so much to say they can't get a word out.

6. This question is a syntax check: it is the "books" (or "looks") that "plead" and "look for recompense."

7. The speaker wants the recipient to use eyes to do what ears would ordinarily do: to sense the depth of love silently conveyed by the speaker's written words (books) or impassioned appearance (looks).

Directed Inquiries

8. "Part" and "books" are everyday words, but also belong

to the professional vocabulary of theater. One possible interpretation of "dumb presagers" is that, like "an unperfect actor," he is capable only of miming emotions he is supposed to be able to express in words.

9. If you know that Shakespeare was an actor, you can easily imagine that he would be familiar with stage fright and forgetting lines. Knowing that he was a great playwright and poet, you may find it hard to believe he would ever be at a loss for words.

10. The images of excessive strength convey the central paradox of the speaker's claim: that he is silent not because he has weak feelings but because his feelings are too strong.

11. The feat of synesthesia shouldn't be difficult since it is characteristic of those who understand love "to hear with eyes."

Analyze

Let the Speaker Guide You to the Meaning: What makes the speaker's behavior "mysterious" is his claim that silence expresses deep feelings. The speaker wants the addressee to accept this claim, to feel adequately loved, and to recognize an obligation to reciprocate this love.

Notice and Account for Metrical Variations: Lines 1-8 are irregular, while lines 9-14 are smoothly iambic. One reason for this might be that in the first eight lines he is trying to explain his failure to speak, and he may find this awkward. In the remaining lines he is making his pitch—asking directly for what he wants from his beloved—and so is more confident about what he wants to say.

Dig Deeper Into Similes: We have already asked these questions about Sonnet 23's similes. This time, try to attach your observations to statements about the poem's meaning. The silence of both an actor and a "fierce thing" is attributable to an excess, not an absence, of emotion. In neither case does the deficiency in speech point to a defect in passion, only to the weakening effect of wanting too deeply or having too much to say.

We discussed "another way to approach . . . similes" in Question 9. Shakespeare was able to depict characters who are unfailingly fluent while in the grip of overwhelming passions—love, anger, terror, misery. As with the actor, we can say either: no, it's inconceivable that the man who provided words to Romeo, Othello, and Macbeth would himself be rendered speechless by his feelings. Or: yes, he must have been able to imagine what it's like to be rendered speechless.

Interpret

The directions provided in the prompt itself should enable you to assemble the pieces you have worked on through the lesson and develop a cogent interpretation. You might look back to the "General Inquiries" (Questions 1 and 2) to get you started with your **paraphrase**, but be sure to look at all the quatrains. For your **explication**, as you consider what the phrases and images mean to the speaker, consider your responses to inquiries about attitude and tone. The "Directed Inquiries" (Questions 9-11) can also make this explication more complete. Finally, as you **evaluate** the speaker's success in explaining his meaning, go back to the section where you analyzed the explanation of the speaker's "mysterious" behavior. Does he effectively convey why this behavior seems mysterious, and why? Why do you think so? Answering these questions and pulling together ideas from throughout the lesson will help you craft a solid interpretation of the poem.

Student Support — Lesson 1

Write About It: As you write this essay, look carefully at what the essay prompt asks for. We have talked at length about the "mysterious" speaker; in this essay, keep your focus on his intention, his desires, and his explanation of his own behavior. Although the question asks you to describe how literary devices work to convey the speaker's dilemma, be sure to remember that these devices are important only insofar as they support what you are saying about the speaker. The suggestion to consider similes, irony, and metrical variation is a **clue**, nudging you into remembering that you have examined these throughout your discussion of the poem. However, the important phrase "such literary devices as" reminds you that other literary elements you have studied may also contribute to the overall meaning.

Lesson 2

A Bird came down the Walk
by Emily Dickinson

Read

Anticipate the Poem: The first line establishes a scene and populates it with an actor (the bird) and, in the second line an observer. The "walk" identifies the setting as one defined by its human uses. The line, "A Bird came down the Walk" also specifies an action, so we will expect, without having to reflect on it, that we are going to be told what the bird did, or what happened to it, as it came down the walk.

First Response: The most obvious difficulties the poem offers up to a first reader are its peculiarities of expression ("in halves . . . ate the fellow raw . . . a dew . . . a convenient grass . . . rapid eyes . . . frightened beads") and the incredibly intricate metaphors of the last few lines. Writing about what it's like to watch an animal should be fun, but there's a payoff too, in noticing that the speaker is doing that.

Respond

Read It Aloud: The important thing here is to let the poem speak itself through you. Even before Dickinson mentions the bird's "rapid" and "hurried" eyes, there is a sense of busy, darting motion. "They looked like frightened beads, I thought" should probably be read slowly and thoughtfully . . . but could also be read with amusement (how absurd a bird!) or pleasure ("How clever of me!"). "He stirred his velvet head" needs to be surrounded by brief silences, so that "Like one in danger, cautious" can stand equally balanced between "he stirred" and "I offered" and can refer either back or forward. At "And he . . ." the voice becomes amazed at the transformation of the bird into a manifestation of the forces of nature. The reading should be quiet, dignified, dazzled. Finally, at "leap plashless as they swim," notice how the unvoiced expulsions of breath on the "p : p" is a perfect analogy for the imperceptible imagined impact of a butterfly on the surface of a pond, and is followed by the effortless glide of "l—sh—l—s." No exaggerated expressiveness is required to permit the speaker's own hushed awe to be felt.

Extended Journal Response: Even at this early stage, you may be able to see that in the first part of the poem the speaker is delightedly watching the bird hopping about, but that when the bird flies away, the speaker is filled with wonder.

Inquire
General Inquiries

1. The speaker has merely offered the bird a crumb, and frightened it away—but the poem presents this as something fraught with meaning.

2. Every reader of Dickinson has to confront her private—though only mildly idiosyncratic—system of punctuation and capitalization. She liked to capitalize nouns, as had once been customary in English and was still in German, and she made the dash do a lot of work. When you know the poem better, look at each of its dashes and try to decide what work it's doing. It may be separating two phrases, marking a transition, indicating a pause either for reaction or reflection, bracketing a parenthetical phrase, creating suspense by delaying a climax, or many other things. Sometimes it's just a dash.

3. We're just calling your attention to something you may have noticed without actually thinking about it: that the observer is as much a character as the bird.

Inquiries about Words and Phrases

4. Dickinson is a master of what came in the twentieth century to be called "the estrangement effect." She asks language to do things no one else asks of it or permits it to do, things no one else would let it. When she does this, we are brought up short and have to look again and think. In this case, she may be trying to see things from the bird's point of view.

5. She may be trying to see things from the bird's point of view. "Dew" and "grass" are collective nouns, but to the bird, they're a drink and a container. And the worm isn't a thing with an existence independent of the bird's intentions, but simply two bites.

6. She may be asking us to recognize and acknowledge how shocking it is that the bird kills and eats its prey—how unlike us.

Inquiries about Attitude and Tone

7. The tone of the first part of the poem can be described in several ways, including *matter-of-fact*, *fascinated*, *amused*, *delighted*, *curious*, and others. The speaker's shock at the bird's behavior has a gently comical effect.

8. The speaker sees herself as a clever and secret observer of a scene that might have been composed expressly for her entertainment. The bird sees itself as just going about its business and, as the poem will make clear in a few lines, regards her as an intruder who spoils everything.

Directed Inquiries

9. At first, all the speaker wants is to watch the bird's delightful performance, but in line 13 she wants the bird to take food from her hand.

10. The conflict might be between the speaker and the bird for control of the story; or between the speaker's sense of herself as a benign presence and the bird's sense that she is an intruder; or between a view of the bird as an amusing performer and as an unfathomable mystery.

11. This question asks you to consider our conventional associations with the idea of a bird in a poem: birds are creatures of the air, graceful fliers, brilliant warblers or cheerful tweeters, delicate feathered friends, afraid of cats and any loud noise, small, dear, anxious, and vulnerable. But when it flies off, it becomes an elegant and unknowable creature of the sky.

12. The speaker is amused (interested, captivated, etc.) by the bird's behavior at first and feels like a naturalist observing the bird, but the sudden elegance and purity of the bird's taking flight is recorded with a sort of enraptured amazement or awe.

13. Although the obvious answer is "the bird," both the punctuation and the break between verses authorize us to think it may be the speaker.

14. She has included an extraordinary number of creatures, habits, and dimensions of nature. See how many you can notice.

Analyze

Fill in the Ellipses: We have to notice that the speaker had gone from wanting simply to observe the bird to wanting to interact with it. and we're never actually told that the bird flies off; we may have to read the poem several times before we realize that this has happened.

Evaluate Imagery: You have already noticed most of these details; now we are asking you to consider their effect on the poem.

Identify metonymy and unpack similes and metaphors:
What makes these lines difficult is the complex texture of the comparisons. They begin by envisioning the bird's ruffling of its wings as an "unrolling" of feathers, and its taking flight as "rowing." This rowing is then compared to oars splitting the surface of the ocean. The infinite air, the bird's native element, is then compared to water.

Interpret

This seemingly simple task is in fact difficult. The poem itself is challenging, and we are asking you to express its subtle and complex ideas in your own words. Can you capture the evolution of the speaker's perception—from amusement to awe?

Write About It: What you are being asked to do here is to examine how the presence of some major poetic elements can lead us to meaning. The imagery of the bird's behavior is conveyed directly in the first 12 lines ("bit . . . ate . . . hopped") but then through figurative language ("unrolled . . . rowed . . . butterflies . . . leap"). Both the bird and the speaker are characterized. And although the poem describes a single experience of watching the bird, the experience itself is in two parts: before and after the speaker offers the bird a crumb.

Lesson 3

The White City
by Claude McKay

Read

Anticipate the Poem: If you don't already know that Claude McKay was a prominent Harlem Renaissance writer, you might not think about race when you look just at the title of "The White City." You might think of "The White City" as it applied to the 1893 Chicago World's Fair, or you might envision white buildings or an imaginative celestial city in the sky. But if you've brainstormed long enough, you have probably thought about "whiteness" as a social construct. In this poem, "The White City" is only attainable only to some—white people. The very process of this brainstorming may prepare you for the emotions and ideas in this poem.

Reading: Although you see that you will "read it aloud" below, it's not a bad idea for your first silent reading to imagine the poem coming through a hate-filled human voice. But think of a slow burn as opposed to an out-of-control rage. Then possibly read it aloud to yourself with the intensely felt hatred you see in the words.

Respond

Journal: Think—and write—with setting and emotion in mind. In your journal, think about your first impression of the title as well as how you revised your first ideas.

Read It Aloud: As stated above in the "Reading" section, this is definitely a poem you will understand better after reading it aloud or hearing it read. It expresses a carefully controlled hate that you should hear in your vocal intonation. A strong tone of yearning should come through in the last six lines, conveying the speaker's reluctant admiration for the city—hatred tinged with longing. Try building volume and vocal intensity on the words evoking the city's grandeur; clipping and punching the final word hate should be chillingly effective.

As you read the poem aloud, be careful, too, not to pause at the ends of lines unless the punctuation suggests it. That is, let each line cross over into the next when there is no end punctuation.

Extended Journal Response: Choosing specific lines or phrases that seem effective or important to you—or even just lines or words you like best—is often a good way to start uncovering a poem's meaning. As you look more closely, you'll see how these phrases and lines connect and work together. For now, just let yourself appreciate and enjoy the phrases and lines that seem to speak to you: phrases where you like how the words work together, lines that say something meaningful in an interesting way, or anything that just seems worth looking in isolation.

Inquire

General Inquiries

1. The speaker is proud of his secret hate; he nurtures and "bear[s] it nobly."

2. The hate is directed toward the great city (New York). The city itself symbolizes the way the white society dominates every aspect of life—social, political, and economic—while excluding the African American speaker. He cannot remember a time when he did not feel this way.

3. The speaker sees and hears:
    - "strident (loud and shrill sounding) trains"

- towering buildings ("poles and spires and towers")
- the harbor
- great ships
- wharves

You should be able to see that all of these connect in different ways to the city's economic dealings. If you think about how all these aspects of the setting reflect the white power structure that controls the economy, you will see where the poem goes next.

Inquiries about Words and Phrases

4. To muse is to "contemplate, ponder, and think about." This may at first seem to be the complete opposite of hate, but in this poem it is not. The speaker's steady contemplation of his hate shows his control; it is part of who he is. The calm hatred is something he thinks deeply about. The double meaning of *muse* also suggests that his hate is his muse; it guides and inspires him.

5. Here are a few of the multiple connotations of dark (you may think of more):

    - evil ("dark side" or "dark intentions")
    - keeping out light ("dark glasses," a "dark room")
    - secret ("in the dark")
    - devoid of light ("dark day")
    - night ("as dark falls")
    - lacking enlightenment (the "Dark Ages")
    - ill humor (a "dark look")
    - having skin with more melanin ("dark-skinned people")

Now apply these to "dark Passion": it is secret, filled with ill humor, and comes from the speaker as he contemplates his role as a Person of Color (that is, "dark") in a society where opportunitues are open only to white people. The capitalization of the word *Passion* emphasizes the depth and power of the speaker's emotion.

6. Wanton also has multiple meanings:

    - "wanton loves": lewd sexual behavior

    - "wanton behavior": occurring without being provoked or for no clear reason

    - wasteful or indulgent

    Thus, the simile "sweet like wanton loves" reveals the speaker's attraction to the city he hates and hints at the pull of the seedy undercurrent of life in the big city. The second meaning—cruelty without provocation—conveys the city's unprovoked rejection of outsiders and minorities.

Inquiries about Attitude and Tone

7. Hate feeds him "vital blood." Without it he would be like a skeleton or empty, cast-off shell. Considering the historical context of the poem, the speaker's hate might even be good
for him—better than just passively accepting injustice and systemic racism.

8. The speaker's wide range of emotions includes:

    - hate

    - anger and determination ("will not toy with it")

    - stubbornness ("will not…bend an inch")

    - stoicism ("without flinch")

    - pride ("bear it nobly")

- sadness ("through a mist…tears")
- admiration for the city
- yearning for respect and acceptance

9. The first eight lines of the poem focus on the speaker's emotions—and the white city is the source of these emotions. The title applies to the whole poem since it is the city that evokes these powerful emotions. The opening lines build up to the description of the majestic city—closed off to the bitter speaker.

Directed Inquiries

10. "It" can have several meanings:
    - the hate the speaker describes
    - the white city
    - the white elite power structure (he won't "toy with it")

11. The line is the opposite of what we might expect: that the glorious city is the white society's heaven and the speaker's hell. Reversing this expectation is more thought-provoking. He celebrates ("heaven") what he ought to find hellish because it is his life-blood, keeping him alive and giving him purpose. This line is also an allusion to a line from William Blake's "The Clod and the Pebble": Love… / …builds a heaven in hell's despair."

12. The speaker seems to be gazing on the city from a distance, just as he is the outsider looking in.

13. You can find both positives and negatives in the images of the city.

    Positives: "poles and spires and towers," "tides," "wharves," "great ships"

Negatives: "strident" (the city's noise), "goaded masses" (the downtrodden people pushed into submission), hate imagery previously discussed.

Analyze

Contemplate the Setting and Its Purpose: McKay's (and his speaker's) hatred is not directed at white people in general but at societal racism. New York City during the 1920s was openly racist, and everything the speaker admires is denied him.

The opening lines relate to the setting because the setting—New York City—has given rise to the speaker's hate (the focus of the opening lines). The title and possibly the opening line also refer to the city and tie it to the concluding lines.

Connect Sonnet Form to Meaning: The Shakespearean sonnet pattern consists of 14 lines in iambic pentameter, divided into three quatrains and a couplet rhyming abab cdcd efef gg.

- The first quatrain defines the speaker's hate and pride in his hate.
- The second quatrain explains how this hate gives him life.
- The third quatrain describes the majestic city.
- The couplet grammatically ties into the third quatrain by continuing to list the city's features.
- Line 14 concludes the poem and connects the ideas from all three quatrains (the usual purpose of the entire couplet).

These strict formal requirements of the sonnet and the poem's lofty, high-toned diction suit the speaker's carefully controlled hate. Most sonnets are love poems, and this one is, too, in its portrayal of the majestic city. It is a love/hate poem: the speaker yearns for the city he would love to love, and in so doing, he holds onto his hate.

Examine Speaker and Tone

The tone clearly embraces the polar opposites of love and hate as you have seen in the sonnet analysis above. This "hate poem" is the antithesis (opposite) of a love poem.

Other examples of antithesis are "wanton loves because I hate" and "heaven in the white world's hell."

Order and restraint are seen in the formal, eloquent diction (as opposed to out-of-control rage). Despite the speaker's resentment and frustration, he finds beauty in his longing for the city, and there is also beauty in the lyrical sonnet form. The speaker does not shout at us (though we wouldn't blame him if he did) but, rather, channels his hatred into creativity and beauty.

Interpret

As you approach the process of interpreting the poem as a whole, go back to the oral reading and look again at the poem line-by-line. At this point, you need to be able to say more than just that the speaker embraces his hate or that the city has led to this hate. Look for more complication and nuance at this point, showing the contradictions and nuances. The speaker's emotional complex, and a thorough interpretation of the entire poem will explore this complexity in detail and with examples from throughout the poem.

Write About It

The speaker's love-hate relationship with the city should form the centerpiece of this prompt. You will want to explore this relationship with a careful analysis of literary elements such as diction, tone, antithesis, and sonnet form.

Lesson 4

The Armadillo
by Elizabeth Bishop

Read

Anticipate the Poem: We don't want to give you any "suggested answers" here yet—that will take away from the very act of anticipating on your part. Just keep thinking about that armadillo; his significance will be clear to you soon enough. In the meantime, one of the best ways to visualize the festival described in this poem is to look up "Festa Junina" and "fire balloons."

Reading: As the lesson itself suggests, think about the tone that the words and descriptions create and how this tone makes us feel. We can almost feel as if we're taking part in the festivities and sharing in the speaker's awe at the beauty she sees. Be sure to focus on the descriptions of the ascending and descending balloons; these will help you understand just where the poem is headed. When the balloons recede from view, the tone (and our resulting response) changes. There is an even more dramatic shift in lines 19-20 with the first mention of danger.

The closing stanza is certainly startling with its sharp change in tone and voice. Bishop signals this jolt clearly by italicizing this stanza and using two exclamation points.

Respond

Journal: Our Fourth of July fireworks suggest bombardment and victory in battle. The fire balloons, while possibly resembling fireworks (vivid against the night sky), are rooted in worship of saints in a predominantly Catholic country. Both practices carry potential for danger and injury though Festa Junina might be even more dangerous.

Read It Aloud: Reading the poem and following the suggestions for emphasis and tone is an important step, whether you are studying this poem in a class or independently.

Extended Journal Response: While firsthand accounts will, of course, vary, this is a good place to begin to see the speaker's ambivalence toward the fire balloons. They are beautiful and breathtaking—but dangerous. Bishop's words permit us to see and feel the devastation, but we are left to formulate our own response.

Inquire

General Inquiries

1. The title helps us identify and empathize specifically with one creature affected by the balloons.

2. The delightfully visual fire balloons almost seem to have a place amidst the natural celestial beauty, but ironically, they destroy the very beauty of the world that the poem's opening celebrates.

3. The "downdraft" catches the balloons in line 19, and the speaker tells us in line 20 that they are "suddenly turning dangerous." The animals in their habitats are most vulnerable.

4. Italics, punctuation, and word choices ("falling fire," "piercing cry," "mailed fist / clenched") make the last stanza much more dramatic. The perspective has shifted dramatically: we are no longer detached but horrified and compassionate. (See also Question 17)

Inquiries about Words and Phrases

5. Other suggestions of frailty and vulnerability:
   - paper chambers (line 7)
   - falter, wobble and toss (line 14)
   - splattered, like an egg (line 22)

   Other balloon traits:
   - colors (pale green, tinted)
   - pulsating lights (flush and fill with light, comes and goes, flare and falter)
   - kinetic aspects (climbing, rising, wobble, steer, receding)

6. Consider the following points:
   - The saint is "in heaven," a state many cultures place in the sky.
   - The word still suggests surprise or hesitation (about the religious aspect).
   - The festival is religious in origin. (See Question 13)
   - Religious elements remain for the highly devout, much as they do at Christmas—possibly the most secularized religious holiday most of us are familiar with.

7. The candles inside the fire balloons are lighted. The flame inside each balloon flickers, thus seeming to "flush" and "come and go" the way candlelight and fire flicker.

8. Most likely these colors represent the reflection of the fire, but some readers might see a suggestion of blood.

9. There is no contest here: the mailed fist can do nothing against the destructive fire and is a "weak mailed

fist" (an oxymoron). The armadillo's shell is the mail (armor).

Inquiries about Attitude and Tone

10. The speaker is awestruck by their beauty and their seemingly majestic place within the heavens.

11. At first, she just observes and describes: she is mildly upset because of the animals in distress, but she is still at arm's length from their fear.

12. The change from the first eight stanzas to the ninth is dramatic and jolting as the shift from observer to victim occurs. Note such words and phrases as "panic" and "piercing cry," as well as the italics and exclamation points.

Directed Inquiries

13. It is deeply ironic that a celebration honoring a saint becomes a vehicle for the destruction of God's natural creation. Are we condoning destruction while professing to be devout? You might also make a connection between the festival and the celebration of Christmas—commercialized and secular despite its religious origins. (See Question 6)

14. The pulsating of the light is like a human heartbeat. When the light "comes and goes like hearts," we are reminded of the often fickle nature of romantic love.

15. The words "last night" alert us to the actual destruction occurring: We see the owls fly away because the fire from the balloon has destroyed their habitat. The armadillo scurrying away and the baby rabbit jumping out confirm the mayhem.

16. The speaker's interruptions let us know that she is taking in several aspects of the scene at once. They establish a sense of chaos and disorder, almost as if she can't keep up with everything happening before her eyes.

17. The speaker at first seems detached and even slightly distracted from the scene. But in the final stanza, we see a sharp contrast from this detachment: she seems horrified and personally affected by what is occurring.

18. The armadillo's outer shell is its "mail," and it serves the same purpose as armor—protection. But it can't protect the vulnerable animal from the devastation that the fire balloons cause. It's also the wrong kind of protection; although the armadillo's covering adapts this animal perfectly for its natural habitat, the shell is as useless as the knight's armor would be in a fire. In the final stanza, we share this perspective and the sense of futility—as we become the helpless armadillo.

19. There are many such forces. Some critics suggest that Bishop is referring to nuclear power and devastation in this poem. Like the powerless animals in the poem, we humans are weak and helpless against the very nuclear weapons we have built.

Analyze

Recognize Shifts in the Speaker's Tone: As the discussion questions above have suggested, the dramatic shift in tone and even speaker in the final stanza cannot be overemphasized. The speaker shifts from detached observer to terrified victim.

We humans are also powerless in the face of much destruction—forest fires, brush fires, and other catastrophes. But unlike the armadillo, we have caused so much of this. Think about the human role in climate change and other ways we have tampered with our earth.

Examine Both Figurative and Concrete Imagery:

- When the balloons "flush and fill with light / …like hearts," they come to life. Our hearts beat along with them.
- The "egg of fire": the flame looks like an egg yolk (visual metaphor).
- The fiery lantern exploding is compared to an egg splattering (kinetic metaphor).
- The rabbit's "intangible ash" is the fire's residue and may also suggest nuclear destruction (like the ashy silhouettes of atomic bomb victims who were once people: look up "Hiroshima shadows" online).
- Concrete color imagery: the owls' "whirling black-and-white," the pink stain (fire's reflection, blood) and the "rose-flecked" shell. (The horrific images of mayhem are as colorful as the bright balloons, but the colors are no longer festive.)

Interpret

As the poem opens, the speaker is detachedly observing, like an anthropologist or maybe an artist: coolly taking in the local customs, noting the natives' beliefs and celebrations, even fussing over which planet is which. Her initial aesthetic appreciation of balloons' beauty shifts to her realization of their destructive power. We see and feel the abrupt change from observation to experience and from thinking to feeling. We humans, too, are subject to destructive forces inside and outside our nature that are appealing, beautiful, and dangerous. You can take this interpretation in many directions. You may see connections to our human exploitation of nature, or you may see the powerless animals as representative of humans threatened by nuclear war.

Write About It: As you write your essay, be sure to follow the speaker from her initial aesthetic appreciation and pleasure in the beauty and celebratory nature of the balloons through her gradual, then sudden, realization of their impact on nature. Explore her changing attitude through shifts in tone, especially the dramatic shift in the final stanza. To write your very best, be sure to weave references to literary devices thoughtfully into your analysis of the speaker's stance. She changes from delighted onlooker to horrified participant who realizes her own complicity in the mayhem. To include the all-important "so what?" element in your essay, show your readers why this matters. To do this, consider any seemingly harmless human activity that leads to ominous results, possibly making relevant connections to the environment or to global (nuclear) threats.

Lesson 5

Aubade
by Philip Larkin

Read

Anticipate the Poem: An "aubade" is a love lyric: you can find a fuller definition in any dictionary of literary terms. This one doesn't seem particularly romantic: Is the title ironic? Or is it appropriate in some other way?

Reading: It's pretty clear that the speaker is meditating our feelings about knowing we will die. Did you notice that the speaker's own self disappears from the poem after dominating the opening lines?

Respond

Read It Aloud: After you've become familiar with "Aubade," read it, or listen to it being read, aloud. How does this experience affect your understanding of, or your feelings about, "Aubade"?

As we hear it, the poem is full of sounds, and the rhyme scheme is complex. The poem's sentences provide the basic rhythmic energy: some of them end at the end of a poetic line, while others run over the ends of the lines. When you come to these (as at lines 6-7, 8-9, 12-13-14-15, 17-18, and many others), read through the line-break with as little hesitation or pause as your eye-skip will permit.

Inquire

General Inquiries

1. The name "aubade" comes from a word that means "dawn," and the aubade is a verse form, developed among the medieval troubadours, in which lovers express their regret at having to part because the dawn has arrived. This one doesn't seem particularly romantic. Is there a sense in which the speaker's realizing he will die someday is like having to say goodbye to a loved one?

2. Obviously, there is no correct answer to these questions. But arguing with the poem's assertions and claims will lead us to examine our own feelings about "dying and being dead."

3. Four AM feels like the perfect hour to be faced with unanswerable questions. It's too early to just get up, but hardly worth going back to sleep.

4. We are asking you to consider from one perspective where your reading has brought you. Do you like the speaker? Dislike him? Feel sorry for him? Agree or disagree with what he says? Identify with or disassociate from his feelings?

Inquiries about Words and Phrases

5. These are questions you may not be ready to answer yet, but they are designed to remind you that interpreting a poem means interpreting all of the poem. The very act of noticing a word or phrase that does not make immediate sense is a crucial step toward a full and correct interpretation. Such words or phrases often point toward meanings that are not apparent at first reading.

6. His basic claim about religion is that it is a "trick," like

logic and being brave; that its purpose is to help us "pretend we never die;" and that we no longer believe it ("used to try"). The specific religion he is referring to here seems to be a form of Christianity that is widely practiced ("vast"), ancient ("moth-eaten"), and characterized by rich liturgy and furnishings ("musical brocade")—perhaps High-Church Anglicanism (Larkin was English).

The poem as a whole is both a thoughtful examination of our fear of death and a spectacular feat of poetic craft, and these metaphors for religion fulfill both of the poet's purposes.

7. This question continues or re-focuses the line of thought opened by the previous question. The proposition "no rational being can fear a thing it will not feel" is "specious," the speaker tells us, because it seems to make sense but turns out on closer examination to be false.

8. Most of the metaphors in "Aubade" can be understood with a little thought. For example, in the phrase "unresting death," death is personified as a creature that never rests; the thought of it "flashes" (line 10) and "glares" (line 11) because thoughts of death may come upon us with unexpected suddenness. But this is a tough metaphor to crack. What did you come up with?

9. Perhaps only to bring us (along with the speaker) back into the daylit world in which there's so much going on—so much activity, so many responsibilities—that we're rescued from the fear of "what's really always there—unresting death."

Inquiries about Attitude and Tone

10. This may seem too obvious to bother with—he spends the whole poem telling us how he feels about death. But

then, what are those feelings? Mostly fear, yes, but that just pushes the question back one level: what is it about death that evokes this fear?

This question may also lead us to ask how the speaker feels about his own life. There's not a lot to work with after that first line, but we do get further glimpses of his feelings.

11. The payoff for focusing on this question is the realization that each verse of "Aubade" has a distinct subject, and that each verse makes an arguable assertion about our response to the idea of death.

12. This question, whose answer no two readers may agree on, nudges us in the direction of a fuller interpretation of the poem as a whole.

Analyze

Pay Careful Attention to Speaker and Point of View: This task ["trace the connection"] develops the ideas we first encountered in trying to answer question 11: that the speaker is both telling us what makes death so terrifying to himself and also projecting those feelings about death onto the reader ("this is what we fear"). Every reader is challenged—or at least invited—to consider whether he or she shares the speaker's feelings and agrees with the speaker's ideas.

Make Metaphors Pay their Way: As with other questions, the intention here is not to evoke a correct answer but to get you thinking about something you might otherwise take for granted. "Of course it's got a lot of metaphors: it's a poem." Yes, but like everything else in the poem—maybe even more so—the metaphors were chosen by the poet, so the question remains, why these metaphors? It's a question about the poet's purposes in writing the poem, and to answer it thoughtfully we will need to offer an account of the various metaphors' effects.

Don't Take Rhyme for Granted: The spectacular elaborateness of the rhyme scheme, somewhat like the virtuosic metaphors, calls attention to the enameled artifice of the poem. It's one of the "sides" that "will have to go."

Interpret

Really, it will be enough if you can address any one of the poem's major challenges. Can you give a complete, coherent summary of the poem's various claims about death? Can you provide a sketch of the speaker's character that reconciles the seemingly contradictory qualities he reveals? Or can you derive from the poem as a whole an idea, feeling, or attitude concerning death that will draw upon all five of its verses?

Write About It: This is perhaps an unusually challenging prompt because two of the suggested poetic elements (rhyme and stanza form) are usually difficult to find much to say about. If you have grappled with Question 11 (on "successive verses") and the Tool Box entry on Rhyme, you should be able to write a strong essay.

THE TOOL BOX

Just as you can use physical tools to help you build or repair something, you can use poetic terminology as a tool to help you discuss and interpret poems. The Tool Box contains brief entries about the technical language of poetry. However, there are two important points to remember—always to remember—about this terminology. First, it is a vocabulary that names ideas rather than things. The second and even more important point is that the ability to name a poetic device is a convenience, not an accomplishment. It is never enough to identify a poetic device. We always need to show how the word, line, or passage we refer to helps us to interpret the poem. Naming the device is simply a shortcut, saving us from a long explanation.

This Tool Box is designed as a supplement to the lessons and a quick resource for you to review and consult terms. Although the Tool Box will occasionally repeat definitions found in other guides, its primary goal is to help you to explore the purposes and application of poetic terms with examples taken directly from the lessons. By applying these examples to the Tool Box section of each lesson, you will ultimately become more comfortable with the language of poetry.

The Tool Box is organized in six sections, each treating one important aspect of poetry and its interpretation. Because these sections attempt to categorize ideas, however, there are important relationships among terms from different categories and occasional overlap from one term to another. Symbol, for example, is a basic literary concept that relates closely to metaphor, a type of figurative language. Categories are merely an attempt to understand what artists and poets do. Just as some songs blend elements of jazz, rock, hip-hop, and blues, so, too, poets' and writers' effects often blur the literary categories. It is helpful to understand these categories—even when innovative artists try to knock down the walls between them.

I. Raw Materials: Basic Literary Concepts 75

   Diction, Speaker and Voice (Point of View), Setting, Symbol, Tone

II. Seeing and Hearing: Imagery and Figurative Language 77

   Conceit, Imagery, Metaphor, Metonymy and Synecdoche, Personification, Simile, Synesthesia

III. Creating Rhythms: Meter and Verse 82

   Free Verse, Metrical Feet, Scansion, Enjambment, Metrical Variation

IV. Presenting Thoughts: Compression and Indirection 86

   Allusion, Ambiguity, Antithesis, Ellipsis, Irony, Paradox and Oxymoron, Parallelism and Repetition, Rhetorical Question

V. The Music and Noise of Poetry: Sound Effects 92

   Alliteration, Consonance, and Assonance, Onomatopoeia, Rhyme

VI. Types of Poetry 94

   Lyric Poetry, Dramatic Monologue, Narrative Poetry

Section I

Raw Materials:
Basic Literary Concepts

Diction

Broadly, diction indicates an author's word choice; more narrowly, it refers to the type of language used in a poem. The word is a convenient one when you want to make a general observation about an author's style. Most poetry before the 1800s was written in a consciously elevated poetic diction—a "poetic" language easily distinguishable from ordinary spoken language or even everyday prose. This elevated diction is still used by poets, but alongside it we have poetry written in language that differs little from conversational English.

Since every word in a poem is chosen, technically every word is diction. But the term is best reserved for moments when it is precisely those chosen words that give the poem its power. When Shakespeare describes blossoms as "the darling buds of May," those exact words capture the delicate, unexpected preciousness of spring's first efforts.

Speaker and Voice (Point of View)

All poems are written in an implied voice. We are listening to someone speaking, and it is this person's voice, not necessarily that of the poet, that we hear. When interpreting poetry, it is customary to refer to the speaker rather than the poet, although in many cases it really is the poet speaking to us. The voice we hear in any given poem is chosen. Poets draw from their lives and emotions, of course, but they also reflect, invent, and create speakers, or personas, whose voices we hear.

Setting

Setting is a major element in fiction and in much nonfiction prose. In poetry, setting—the scene the poet creates—can be important in one of two ways. Many poems are about a place: McKay's "The White City," for example. The poets describe what they see in these places and may also reflect on the ideas or feelings that come to them in the places. Or setting may present an occasion for reflection: What is important is not the scene itself but what happens there.

Symbol

A symbol is something that stands for something else. We encounter symbols constantly—traffic signs and team logos are familiar examples. In a literary work, however, a symbol is something that is both itself and something bigger or greater than itself. When William Blake talks about the human body in "The Divine Image," he means the human body, its beauty and expressiveness. But he also asks us to take the human body as symbolizing, or standing for, something greater: the image of God.

Tone

Tone refers to the speaker's or poet's attitude, and is communicated through the speaker's voice. In a literal sense, the tone of the poem is an idea about how it would sound if we heard the poet reading it—which is to say how we think we should read it.

Section II
Seeing and Hearing: Imagery and Figurative Language

Conceit

Many poetic comparisons are effective because they are so appropriate. A conceit is a comparison that works in the opposite direction. Instead of thinking, "That's so true!" we ask, "How is the poet ever going to make this work?" Conceits tend to be far-fetched, shocking, and elaborate. They will often extend over long passages of a poem or a whole poem. The most famous conceit in English poetry occurs in "A Valediction: Forbidding Mourning" when Donne compares the parted lovers to the legs of a draftsman's compass. Shakespeare's comparison of his beloved to a summer's day may be considered a conceit in two senses. It is highly elaborated, extending through the poem's first twelve lines. And it is shocking because it actually says "you are not like a summer's day: you are much nicer than that."

Imagery

One of poetry's most important powers is its ability to convey vivid and memorable sense impressions. When these impressions are conveyed through comparisons, they are classified as figurative language (metaphor, simile, or personification). But when something is being described in terms of itself—what it looks, tastes, smells, sounds, and feels like—it is called imagery. Dickinson, in "A Bird came down the Walk," perfectly captures the way a bird alighting on the ground pecks, hops about, and swivels its neck alertly.

Metaphor

A **metaphor** is a direct comparison or equation between two unlike things. It describes or characterizes something in terms of another thing. Metaphor is the most basic form of poetic statement and may almost be said to define poetry itself. Of course, metaphor is also an element of ordinary speech. When we say "my mother is an angel" or "if I don't pass that test tomorrow, I'm toast," we are straying into poetry. Metaphors allow the poet to make emotional, visual, psychological, or moral statements without logical arguments or elaborate explanations.

When the speaker in "The Armadillo" describes the rabbit as "a handful of intangible ash," she compares it to something very unlike a rabbit. Any reader of poetry will encounter metaphors like this one constantly and needs to be ready to run with them rather than fight them off. They will be found in virtually every poem in this book and will almost always be one of the keys to the poem's meaning. In "A Bird came down the Walk," the bird is compared to a rower. In both of these cases, our effort to trace the appropriateness of the metaphors will bring us very near to the heart of the poem. Simply asking, "How is a rabbit like a pile of untouchable ash?" or "How is a bird taking off like a person rowing?" gets us thinking along with the poem and is always the right way to go.

Metonymy and Synecdoche

Metonymy and synecdoche are figures of speech, ways of talking about something indirectly. Metonymy offers something associated with or representative in place of the thing that is actually being talked about. We are familiar with this figure from the daily news: "Capitol Hill," where Congress meets, stands for the legislative branch of government, and "Wall Street," home to the New York Stock Exchange, stands for the entire United States stock market. In Shakespeare's Sonnet 116, "rosy lips and cheeks" stand for youth, which is ideally characterized by a fresh, glowing complexion. Blake's "London" offers a series of metonymies such as "Church" in place of organized religion, and "Palace walls" in place of the power of government.

Synecdoche works in a similar manner, but it substitutes a part of something for the whole thing. When we ask someone to "lend us a hand," we are really asking them to help us, and not with just one hand. The "eyes, lips, and hands" that Donne's lovers will not miss in "A Valediction: Forbidding Mourning" represent the physical presence of whole bodies—what other lovers require if they are to go on loving.

Metonymy and synecdoche can overlap: When "Mrs Lazarus" registers "the shock / of a man's strength under the sleeve of [the schoolteacher's] coat," we can call this metonymy because the man's arm is associated with his health and vitality. But we could also call it synecdoche: his arm stands for his whole, healthy, living self. Similarly, Donne's "eyes, lips, and hands" are also metonymic. It isn't those parts of a person in themselves that are missed. What is really missed is the looking, kissing, and touching that they do.

Personification

Personification is the familiar figure of speech in which a nonhuman entity—an animal, a natural phenomenon, or an abstract concept—is written about as if it had human emotions or intentions. Personification is an almost unnoticed resource in ordinary language. We refer to "ol' man winter," picture death as "the grim reaper," imagine love as an arrow-shooting cherub, and refer to a balky machine as "having a mind of its own."

Personification is the organizing principle of Wordsworth's "Composed on Westminster Bridge." The city is seen as wearing the beauty of the morning "like a garment." The river, unoccupied by commercial traffic, glides "at his own sweet will." And "the very houses seem asleep." In Keats' "Ode on Melancholy," the emotional sensations of beauty, joy, and pleasure are depicted as living in proximity to each other. Melancholy itself is portrayed as a sort of hunter or collector of souls, which she displays as trophies. Often personification is introduced casually, in implied metaphors. In the three Shakespeare sonnets, for example, summer is seen as a renter and death as a braggart in Sonnet 18, heaven is deaf in Sonnet 29, and time is a reaper, harvesting youthful good looks, in Sonnet 116.

Simile

Like a metaphor, a simile is a comparison of two unlike objects for artistic or rhetorical purposes. The distinguishing feature of the simile is its use of like or as to introduce the comparison. Frost's "Design" contains several similes that function as snapshots. They document the scene the speaker is observing and its impact on him: "Like a white piece of . . . satin cloth," "Like the ingredients of a witches' broth," "A flower like a froth," and "like a paper kite." In Dickinson's "A Bird came down the Walk" the simile is explicitly an immediate impression: the bird's eyes "looked like frightened Beads, I thought." Heaney's speaker compares the pen in his hand to a weapon: "snug as a gun." But a simile can also convey a powerfully complex image, as when Donne tries to indicate that separation is not separation in "A Valediction: Forbidding Mourning." He captures this idea—that the lovers, though far apart, remain attached to each other—by comparing them to gold that has been hammered to a foil ("Like gold to airy thinness beat").

It is important to remember than not every use of like or as constitutes a simile. In Sonnet 29, for example, when Shakespeare says that the awakening of his soul is "Like to the Lark at break of day arising," he's created a simile. But when, in the same poem, he wishes he were "like to one more rich in hope," he literally wishes he could be a more hopeful person.

Synesthesia

In science and medicine, synesthesia refers to a neurological condition in which the senses are linked. People with this condition really do experience one sense through another. This unusual phenomenon has also crept into our everyday language in such synesthetic expressions as "loud colors" and "smooth jazz." Poets, too, draw from this extraordinary condition; they blend the senses or describe the experience of one sense in terms of another. When Shakespeare writes "Sometime too hot the eye of heaven shines" in Sonnet 18, he triggers our senses by describing a blending of heat (touch) and light from the sun. Dickinson's "There's a certain Slant of light" owes much of its poetic power to its almost continual synesthesia: light that weighs down (oppresses), tunes that have heft (weight), landscapes that listen, and shadows that breathe. Bishop's "The Map" blends the senses of sight and hearing, with "Mapped waters are more quiet than the land is." And in Blake's "London," the synesthesia horrifyingly blends sound and sight in "the hapless Soldier's sigh / Runs in blood down Palace walls."

Section III

Creating Rhythms:
Meter and Verse

Free Verse

Free verse is one of the main techniques for organizing a poem, especially in the poetry of the last hundred years. Before that time, most poetry was organized either in stanzas, in blank verse (unrhymed iambic pentameter), or in "fixed forms," poetic forms, like the sonnet, with a prescribed pattern of rhyme, meter, and line lengths. Free verse is "free" in not being organized by any regular pattern of meter, rhyme, or line. But it is also "verse" in that it is organized—by breath, by sound, by the unit of sense, or by the rhythms of ordinary speech.

Although Robert Frost compared writing free verse to "playing tennis without a net," the modern free-verse poet might reply that writing free verse is more demanding than writing rhymed, metric poetry. It does not provide a readymade template, so the modern free-verse poet is entirely on his or her own when generating a poem. In "Theme for English B," free verse permits Hughes to mimic the stops and starts of a college freshman trying to outline a paper. In "Introduction to Poetry," it enables Collins to present a whole series of quick ideas about poetry almost the way a magician pulls scarves out of his or her sleeve. And in "Mrs Lazarus," free verse allows Duffy to reproduce the gasping rhythm of a woman recovering her breath after a violent bout of weeping.

Metrical Feet

Meter refers to repeated patterns of stressed and unstressed syllables in each line of poetry. The term metrical foot (or feet) is used to describe each individual unit of stresses. There are four common metrical feet: iambic, trochaic, anapestic, and dactylic. Of these, iambic is by far the most frequently used meter in English poetry. Metrical feet are usually illustrated with a forward slash mark over the accented beat and a cup-shaped mark, like a u, over the unaccented beat, but in this book the stressed syllables will be indicated with upper-case letters. Here are examples of words that represent each foot:

Iambic: deny, delight   (Say it: de-NY, de-LITE)

Trochaic: earring, pancake   (Say it: EAR-ring, PAN-cake)

Anapestic: unimpressed, violin (Say it: un-im-PREST, vi-uh-LIN)

Dactylic: harmony, victory   (Say it: HAR-muh-nee, VIK-tuh-ree)

We also have words, based on Latin roots, for the number of feet in each line:

monometer = one foot   hexameter = six feet

dimeter = two feet   heptameter = seven feet

trimeter = three feet   octameter = eight feet

tetrameter = four feet   nonometer = nine feet

pentameter = five feet

These terms are tools for you to determine metrical schemes. (See *scansion*.)

Scansion

Scansion, or scanning, refers to what we do when we look at a line of poetry to determine its metrical scheme—the type and number of feet. For example, if the meter is anapestic, and there are three feet of anapests, we say that the line is anapestic trimeter. The line "Between my finger and my thumb" in Seamus Heaney's "Digging" is iambic (be-TWEEN), and we can count four of these iambs (be-TWEEN / my FIN /-ger AND / my THUMB) so this line is iambic tetrameter, though "and" may not be pronounced as emphatically as the other accented words. Langston Hughes' "Ballad of the Landlord" opens with a pounding trochaic dimeter: LAND-lord / LAND-lord, (repeated later: PRE-cinct STA-tion and COP-per's WHIS-tle).

This book includes only a few examples of the possible combinations of meter and feet. Many of the book's poems are in free verse and do not have a regular meter. Several poems and almost all the sonnets are written in iambic pentameter, the meter that sounds closest to normal English speech patterns. Here are some examples of metrical schemes from the poems in this book:

"Introduction to Poetry": or PRESS / an EAR / a-GAINST / its HIVE (iambic tetrameter)

Sonnet 18: But THY / e-TER- / -nal SUM - / -mer SHALL / not FADE (iambic pentameter)

"There's a certain Slant of light": WE can / FIND no / SCAR" (trochaic trimeter)

(Emily Dickinson's poems use common measure, in which the lines alternate trochaic tetrameter—which we see in the title line—and trochaic trimeter, as in this line.)

Unvarying metrical patterns are generally found only in doggerel, bad greeting card verse, or advertising jingles. The importance of metrical schemes is not that they exist but how they impact the sound and mood of poetry. Accomplished poets recognize that an unvarying pattern can sound stilted and forced.

Enjambment

Enjambment, the continuation of a poetic sentence from one line to another, comes from a French word that means "striding over" because the sentence or unit of thought straddles more than one line. Enjambment directs us to keep reading without a pause at the ends of unpunctuated poetic lines. Wordsworth's "Composed Upon Westminster Bridge, September 3, 1802" includes these enjambed lines, among others: "Never did sun more beautifully steep / In his first splendour, valley, rock, or hill." A pause after "steep" will interrupt the meaning that the sun "steep[s] . . . valley, rock or hill."

Metrical Variation

Metrical variation refers to any metrical foot that differs from the dominant meter in a line of poetry. Slight metrical variations will almost always be found in good poetry. Although we usually ignore these and label the meter and line length that predominate, inventive poets can startle us with more noteworthy variations. For these cases, which can have a strong impact on a poem's meaning and mood, we have some specific labels. A spondee is a foot (like an iamb or trochee—see Metrical Feet on page 135) consisting of two stressed syllables that interrupt an otherwise regular meter. Hopkins' "Spring and Fall" contains spondaic phrases, such as "will weep" and "ghost guessed," which heighten the poem's mood of loss vocally by emphasizing both words, as well as by alliteration. An alexandrine, a line of iambic hexameter, concludes every stanza of Donne's "The Good Morrow," possibly to emphasize with these overflowing, longer lines the abundance of love conveyed throughout the poem.

Section IV

Presenting Thoughts:
Compression and Indirection

Allusion

An allusion is an indirect reference to a mythological, Biblical, or literary text or character, or to a historical or current event or figure. Allusions both enrich a poem and affirm the common cultural heritage of poet and reader. Some allusions are obvious: Duffy's "Mrs Lazarus" alludes to a Biblical story most readers will recognize. Other allusions may be drawn from less familiar sources, like Donne's reference to "the seven sleepers" in "The Good Morrow," which refers to a nowforgotten legend. Other allusions may just be suggested: "the blight man was born for" in "Spring and Fall" by Hopkins probably refers to the doctrine of original sin. And "the black river of loss" in Oliver's "In Blackwater Woods" may allude to one of the rivers of death that ran into Hades.

Ambiguity

An expression that can be interpreted in more than one sense, or whose meaning cannot be established with certainty, is ambiguous. Poetry is largely an art of ambiguity: meanings and emotions gather in the gap between expression and comprehension.

Ambiguity can be created by words that have more than one commonly accepted meaning. This is the case in Donne's "Valediction," where "reckon" (line 10) means both "add up a column of figures" and "take a guess." Sometimes ambiguity is the result of ellipsis, which is the omission of connective or explanatory words (see ellipsis). Frost's "Desert Places" offers this sort of ambiguity in the line "The woods around it have it—it is theirs." He never tells us what "it" is. At other times, however, ambiguity is just a general effect of language that is too indirect, complicated, or strange to permit immediate understanding. For example, Bishop's "The Map" contains these ambiguous lines: "We can stroke these lovely bays, / under a glass as if they were expected to blossom, / or as if to provide a clean cage for invisible fish."

Ambiguity is generally avoided in ordinary speech and writing, where our aim is to be understood, but it is a powerful tool in the hands of a poet. It causes us to pause and think. This is the basic goal of Collins's "Introduction to Poetry," where none of the poem's statements makes strict literal sense but each reveals another facet of poetry's power to delight or amaze us.

Antithesis

Antithesis is the expression of directly opposed or strongly different ideas in grammatically balanced phrases. It can create a witty effect, as in Frost's "Mending Wall" when he asks "Isn't it / Where there are cows? But here there are no cows," and "I'd ask to know / What I was walling in or walling out." Similarly, we are both struck by the cleverness and moved by the pathos of Hughes' plaintive question and answer in "Theme for English B": "So will my page be colored that I write? / Being me, it will not be white." At other times, antithesis may create a rhythmic effect like breathing, as in "There's a certain Slant of light" in the lines that begin "When it comes..." and "When it goes..." (Lines 13, 15) Antithesis is frequently encountered in Shakespeare's sonnets and Donne's lyrics in this book. Shakespeare will use antithesis to sharpen a contrast, as in "With what I most enjoy contented least," (Sonnet 29, line 8) and "Whose worth's unknown, although his height be taken" (Sonnet 116, line 8). Donne's "Valediction" is structured as a continuous antithesis between the love of ordinary lovers ("the laity") and that of Donne and his beloved who, it is implied, are initiates in the deeper mysteries of love.

Ellipsis

Ellipsis is the poetic technique of omitting a word or words required by grammar or sense. It is a basic element of poetic compression that asks the reader to insert the needed words. It is an especially important resource for modern poets. In "Because I could not stop for Death," Dickinson writes, "only Gossamer, my Gown— / My Tippet—only Tulle—," omitting the "was" from each of those descriptions. The line "None may teach it—Any" in "There's a certain Slant of light" is even more elliptical, since we cannot be sure what words might provide the missing sense. Nye's "Daily" depends on ellipsis—it postpones the predicate for the poem's entire length. This is in keeping with her assertion that "The days are nouns." She names and characterizes all the things she handles during her day, but never tells us what she wants to say about them.

Irony

The word irony derives from a Greek word for "deception" and is appropriately difficult to define. In general we can say that irony depends on a discrepancy. The discrepancy may develop between what is intended or expected and the results, between what is said and what is meant or understood, or between what seems to be true and what is actually the case. This last sort of irony is apparent in "Mending Wall," where two neighbors affirm their neighborliness by performing an act of mutual exclusion: repairing the wall that separates their properties. The ghastly irony of "Mrs Lazarus" lies in that poem's overturning our confident expectation that a woman who was grief-stricken by her husband's death will be overjoyed to learn he has been restored to life. There is sly irony in the seemingly innocent question asked by the speaker of "Theme for English B": "Will my page be colored that I write?" Since we read poetry with heightened alertness to shades of meaning, irony can be especially effective in poetry.

Paradox and Oxymoron

Paradox and oxymoron offer contradictions that allow poets to highlight their ideas. A paradox is a statement or situation that seems to contradict itself, sometimes even to the point of absurdity. In poetry, such contradictions can offer insights into life, contradictions that are often profound, occasionally angry or biting, and sometimes light or ironic. Dickinson's "There's a certain Slant of light" is filled with paradox, beginning with the speaker's gloomy response to light, something we usually associate with cheerfulness. The abundant synesthesia in the poem is also paradoxical: cathedral tunes that oppress, a landscape that listens, and shadows that hold their breath, among others. All of these phrases offer insights into the speaker's mood and remind us that depression involves all our senses and is physical as well as emotional. The closing line of McKay's "The White City" is similarly paradoxical as the speaker describes New York City's features as "sweet like wanton loves because I hate." The paradox of a hate fueled by love causes us to look thoughtfully at our country's disturbing legacy of racism.

Oxymoron, a pairing of opposites, can be considered a compressed paradox. The phrases "Cathedral Tunes" and "Heavenly Hurt" in "There's a certain Slant of light" continue the paradoxical thrust of the entire poem in compressed phrases. An oxymoron can startle and even shock us, as it does in the closing phrase of William Blake's "London," the "Marriage hearse."

Parallelism and Repetition

Parallelism and repetition are similar but distinguishable rhetorical devices for emphasizing an idea or impression. In both cases, a word or phrase is mentioned several times. Parallelism, however, requires that the phrasing be identical, or at least grammatically parallel in each case. A familiar example of parallelism is the phrase "I have a dream" in the famous speech by Martin Luther King, Jr. Both repetition and parallelism can be used to balance contrasting or opposed ideas in identical or near-identical phrases. They can also be used to hammer home a point or to create a unified thread of meaning. In Shakespeare's Sonnet 29, the elegantly balanced parallelism of "Desiring this man's art, and that man's scope, / With what I most enjoy contented least" conveys the completeness of the speaker's despair: There's no person he can look on without envy and no pleasure he can indulge in without aggravating his depression. In Blake's "London," the parallel expressions "How the Chimney-sweeper's cry," "And the hapless Soldier's sigh," and "How the youthful Harlot's curse" add up to a powerful indictment of the economic and social order. In the same poem, however, "chartered," "mark," "cry," and "every" are repeated eleven times in the poem's first seven lines without conspicuous parallelism. Their weary repetition is like the tolling of a funeral bell.

In Blake's "The Divine Image," the words "mercy," "pity," "peace," and "love" occur five to six times, but only the first three are in parallel form. We can have little doubt of what the poem is about. The powerful conclusion of "In Blackwater Woods" is achieved through the repetition of a simple four-word phrase, "to let it go," which has in context two significantly different meanings. Rhyme and meter, the most noticeable elements in traditional poetry, lend themselves easily to repetition and parallelism and support them fully. Because of this, most poems will contain at least a strong hint of parallelism and repetition. As with imagery and figurative language, tracing a poem's repeated or parallel elements will often bring us deep into its meaning.

Rhetorical Question

Simply put, a rhetorical question is one that doesn't expect an answer. It is called "rhetorical" because such questions are a tool of rhetoric; that is, writing based on reasoning and argumentation. Rhetorical questions in poetry often provide a powerful key to meaning. If an idea is significant enough for the poet to pose it as a question, it usually offers important food for thought. The poet is pushing us to muse about something, as Bishop does when she asks about the colors of a map: "Are they assigned, or can the countries pick their colors?" Hopkins' "Spring and Fall" opens with two successive rhetorical questions: Márgarét, áre you gríeving / Over Goldengrove unleaving? / Leáves, líke the things of man, you / With your fresh thoughts care for, can you?" The speaker doesn't expect Margaret to answer him: he poses the questions to set the stage for a meditation on loss.

Section V

The Music and Noise of Poetry:
Sound Effects

Alliteration, Consonance, and Assonance

Alliteration, consonance, and assonance all rely on repetition of sounds and take us back to nursery rhymes and tongue twisters. Alliteration, the repetition of beginning sounds, is heard in the phrase "Bessie, bop, or Bach" in Hughes' "Theme for English B." Within the same phrase, "bop, or Bach" provides assonance, as do many other lines in this poem (for example, "feel . . . see . . . hear . . . me . . . we"). These assonant words have the same vowel sounds, and refer to both the African American student and his white professor, emphasizing the connection between them. Consonance, closely related to alliteration, emphasizes the repetition of consonant sounds, though not necessarily at the beginnings of words. Notice the repetition of k sounds in a line from Shakespeare's Sonnet 29: "Like to the Lark at break of day arising." The crisp k sounds emphasize how thoughts of love have perked up the speaker's spirits. Donne weaves alliteration and assonance throughout "The Apparition" in lines such as "And that thou thinkst thee free." Repeated short a sounds ("and that"), repeated th sounds ("that thou thinkst thee") and repeated long e sounds ("thee free") overlap in a sharply focused warning perfect for the would-be ghost.

Onomatopoeia

Onomatopoeia refers to words that make the sounds they describe. When you say the words aloud, you can actually hear what is being described, as you do with simple examples like pop, buzz, and shush. In Duffy's "Mrs Lazarus," we hear the sounds of grief in the first stanza through the onomatopoeic words howled and shrieked. In Hopkins' "Spring and Fall," the word sigh, especially within the alliterative phrase "spare a sigh," adds to the mournful effect. We hear the sound of sighing again in Donne's neologism, or invented word, sigh-tempests in "A Valediction: Forbidding Mourning." In the same poem we hear whisper, a particularly effective choice in a stanza that discusses breath leaving the body.

Rhyme

It is seldom necessary to refer to rhyme when interpreting a poem. However, recognizing types of rhyme and rhyme schemes can help you as you explore the structure of a poem, and often structure provides a key to meaning. We have special names for rhymes depending on where they occur. End rhyme, obviously, refers to rhymes that occur at the ends of lines, as seen in Blake's "London" and Hughes' "Ballad of the Landlord." Rhyme within lines, internal rhyme, is found in Hughes' "Theme for English B." Masculine rhyme refers to end rhymes on the stressed syllable, like heat and street in "Ballad of the Landlord." Feminine rhyme endings are double rhymes ending on the unstressed syllable, such as grieving and unleaving in Hopkins' "Spring and Fall." Rhymes that are close but not exact have a variety of names, including slant rhyme, near rhyme, and eye rhyme. These not-quite rhymes are found in "The Divine Image" and in much of Emily Dickinson's poetry. The pattern of rhyme in structured poems (such as sonnets and ballads) is called a rhyme scheme. Rhyme scheme is denoted with the use of repeated lower case letters, such as abab or abcb. (See the Tool Box section of "Desert Places," Lesson 11, for additional discussion of rhyme schemes.)

Section VI

Types of Poetry

Lyric Poetry

The term lyric means "songlike." The most common form of poetry, lyric poetry expresses and evokes individual, personal emotion. The introspection of Frost's "Desert Places," the exuberance of Collins' "Introduction to Poetry," and the philosophical reflections of Oliver's "In Blackwater Woods" are all characteristic of lyric poetry. An ode, like Keats' "Ode on Melancholy" is a specific type of lyric intended to honor and exalt its subject.

Another specific type of lyric is the sonnet (literally, "short song"), a 14-line poem with a specific structure and meter. Traditionally, sonnets were divided into two types: Italian, or Petrarchan (named in honor of Petrarch, its most famous practitioner), and English, or Shakespearean. A Petrarchan sonnet, such as Frost's "Design," is divided into two sections: an eight-line octave and a six-line sestet. The octave's rhyme scheme is abba abba, while the sestet rhymes cdecde or a cdcdee. The Petrarchan form can effectively treat subjects that can be looked at in two ways, such as before and after, compare and contrast, or question and answer.

The Shakespearean sonnet is generally organized into three quatrains (four line verses) in alternating rhymes—abab cdcd efef—with a concluding rhymed couplet, gg. The quatrains examine a question or state of affairs that has three elements (4-4-4). The couplet summarizes, resolves, or sometimes contradicts what has been said earlier in the poem. In Shakespeare's Sonnet 29, the quatrains focus on three aspects of the poet's sense of dejection: its intensity, its effect on his attitude toward other people, and the cheering effect of knowing he is loved. The couplet affirms the power of love to banish depression. A sonnet requires of the poet two contradictory powers: the power to compress a complex idea into a mere fourteen lines and the power to sustain a single feeling for a full fourteen lines. The sonnet demands a sprinter's speed and a distance runner's endurance. It is an ideal vehicle for communicating powerful emotions in poetry.

Dramatic Monologue

In a dramatic monologue, a single speaker presents a small drama in a poem. A persona, or speaker, who is clearly not the poet, tells his or her story. As in stage drama, an audience is implied and a setting is established. In "Mrs Lazarus," Duffy speaks through the assumed voice of a fictitious, imagined woman. "Spring and Fall" by Hopkins has been called a dramatic monologue by some critics who believe the speaker would not express his harsh truths to a young child. And in Donne's "The Apparition," the speaker insinuates disturbing and frightening ideas into the mind of his beloved by threatening that his ghost will visit her in bed when she is with a new lover.

Narrative Poetry

Narrative poetry is poetry that narrates or tells a story. Like short stories and novels, narrative poems may have a plot, characters, setting, theme, and point of view. In Frost's "Mending Wall," the speaker tells us a story about repairing fences that turns into a philosophical argument. Dickinson's "Because I could not stop for Death" evokes emotion through its fantastical narrative of personified death driving a carriage toward "eternity." The ballad is a traditional form of narrative poetry. Troubadours who traveled from town to town sang the earliest folk ballads. Literary ballads, like Hughes' "Ballad of the Landlord," are conscious imitations of folk ballads by known poets and are also often set to music.

ABOUT THE AUTHORS

Martin Beller, Ph.D.

Martin Beller is a Visiting Assistant Professor in the English Department at Texas Southern University. He has also taught at The Ohio State University, New York Institute of Technology, New York University and Long Island University, and at YES Preparatory Public School. He received his B.A. in English and Philosophy from C.W. Post College in New York and his M.A. and Ph.D. from The Ohio State University, concentrating on Medieval and Renaissance Literature. His dissertation was a history of the editing of Shakespeare from 1709 to 1863.

Dr. Beller has published articles and reviews and delivered conference papers on Chaucer and the Gawain-Poet, Shakespeare and Marlowe, the nineteenth-century novel, and contemporary film. He served as a Consultant on the *Shakespeare Skillbook* series written by Barbara Bloy and Donna Tanzer, and has also served as a Reader and Table Leader for the AP English Literature and Composition exam.

Donna Carlson Tanzer, M.A.

Donna C. Tanzer is an Adjunct Professor of Writing and Humanities at the Milwaukee Institute of Art & Design (MIAD), where she teaches a wide range of courses including metafiction, children's literature, and fairy tales. She has also taught graduate education courses at Marian University in Fond du Lac, Wisconsin. She formerly taught AP English Literature and many more high school classes in West Allis, Wisconsin, where she also directed over 25 plays, including Shakespearean comedies and an original adaptation of *Pride and Prejudice*.

Ms. Tanzer earned a B.S. in English and Speech (theatre emphasis) from the University of Minnesota—Duluth and an M.A. in Education from Marian University. She has been an AP Reader in English Literature and Composition for the College Board since 2004. She wrote *Teacher's Guide for the Advanced Placement Program* to accompany Kirzner and Mandell's *Literature: Reading, Reacting, Writing* (2013), published by Cengage, and was formerly the lead writer for several editions of *Perrine's Literature: Teacher's Guide for the Advanced Placement Program* (2007, revised and expanded 2009-2014, Cengage), co-authored with Claudia Klein Felske. Ms. Tanzer and Dr. Beller also co-wrote *Interpreting Poetry: Classic and Contemporary Poems* (Peoples Education, 2010). With Barbara Bloy, Ms. Tanzer co-authored four *Shakespeare Skillbooks* on *Macbeth*, *King Lear*, *Hamlet*, and *Othello*, also published by Peoples Education (2009). Other publications include contributions to the *Utah English Journal* and articles for two volumes of the College Board's AP Literature and Composition Professional Development Workshop Materials.

Ms. Tanzer and Dr. Beller have co-presented several workshops on teaching poetry at the Advanced Placement Annual Conference in 2009 and 2010, and at the NCTE annual convention in 2009. Ms. Tanzer also presented at APAC Conferences in 2008 and 2011.

ACKNOWLEDGMENTS

Author Acknowledgments

I would like to thank my dear friend Donna Tanzer for inviting me to share this work. Dixie Gibbs Dellinger and I have been discussing poems for nearly ten years, and her love of poetry and of teaching are invisible but crucial parts of each of my lessons. My present and past students served uncomplainingly as guinea pigs for several of these lessons, and my colleagues in the English Department at YES Preparatory Public School offered valuable feedback. My friends and fellow teachers Mukti Dave, Stefan Fleischer, Michael Glazner, Ruthie Johnson, Michael Morris, Nancy Reddy, and Leigh Anne Rayburn kindly read early drafts of some of the lessons and helped me improve them.

–Martin Beller

Writing this book has been an unforgettable journey of poetic exploration and discovery for me. Among its most joyful aspects has been the opportunity to examine poetry with my dear friend Martin Beller, whose literary insights are always a treasure. I am grateful for the support of my colleagues and students at the Milwaukee Institute of Art and Design as well as that of my sister, Diane Endorf, and many good friends, fellow writers, and former colleagues, especially Jill Carroll, Lynn Clark, Claudia Felske, Velda Iverson, and Susan Mathews. The students I've taught throughout the years have inspired me to remember that the real goal of any teaching is to guide young people as they become thoughtful, insightful adults and professionals, and I've taken this reminder to heart with everything I've written in this book.

Finally, I thank my loving husband, Paul Tanzer, for just about everything—for listening to my concerns, sharing my ideas, offering cogent suggestions, and above all, for believing in me.

–Donna Tanzer

Publisher's Acknowledgments

Sherpa Learning gratefully acknowledges the high school English teachers who reviewed a prototype and provided valuable insights that helped to shape this book.

Reprinted by permission of Harvard University Press:

THE POEMS OF EMILY DICKINSON: READING EDITION, edited by Ralph W. Franklin, Cambridge, Mass.: The Belknap Press of Harvard University Press, Copyright © 1998, 1999 by the President and Fellows of Harvard College. Copyright © 1951, 1955 by the President and Fellows of Harvard College. Copyright © renewed 1979, 1983 by the President and Fellows of Harvard College. Copyright © 1914, 1918, 1919, 1924, 1929, 1930, 1932, 1935, 1937, 1942 by Martha Dickinson Bianchi. Copyright © 1952, 1957, 1958, 1963, 1965 by Mary L. Hampson.

Reprinted by permission of Farrar, Straus and Giroux:

"The Armadillo" from POEMS by Elizabeth Bishop. Copyright © 2011 by The Alice H. Methfessel Trust. Publisher's Note and compilation copyright © 2011 by Farrar, Straus and Giroux. "Aubade" from THE COMPLETE POEMS OF PHILIP LARKIN by Philip Larkin, edited by Archie Burnett. Copyright © 2012 by The Estate of Philip Larkin.

Sherpa Learning, LLC. has made every effort to obtain permission for the reprinting of all selections contained herein. If any author is not acknowledged, please contact the publisher for proper acknowledgment in all future editions or reprintings of this book.

ALSO AVAILABLE FROM SHERPA LEARNING

5-MINUTE DRILL

by Rich Mayorga, Ed.S.

The 5-Minute Drill is an easy and effective way to answer challenging questions with an organized essay that makes an insightful interpretation and claim, contains evidence to support it, and provides a strong analytical explanation. The 5MD process is based around a simple, student-generated graphic organizer with clear diagnostic capabilities. In class, the 5MD can be used at the end of each topic or concept to review and connect content items into a quick, well-integrated essay outline. Each step in the process is supported with examples from both World and U.S. History that each contain a prompt and sample thesis sentence. Also included are essential tips, sample drills, sample essays, additional practice prompts, and guidance on extending the drill to literary and rhetorical analysis. Grades 7-12. 100 p.

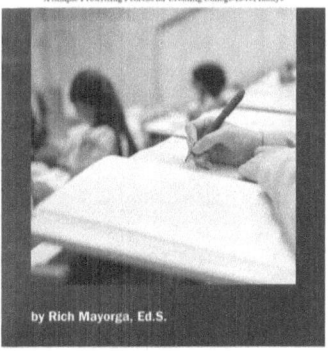

| **ISBN:** | 978-1-948641-17-3 (print) | list: $15.00 | bulk: $10.00 |
| | 978-1-948641-18-0 (ebook) | list: $ 8.00 | bulk: $ 6.00 |

Also Available from Sherpa Learning

Mastering DOCUMENT ANALYSIS

by Tony Maccarella

FINDING THE PAST IN 3 SIMPLE STEPS

Analyzing primary sources vastly expands your understanding of important historical events, while also promoting the development of high-level critical thinking skills. *MDA* presents you with a simple and effective 3-step approach to extract information from primary and secondary source documents so that you can make a deep and meaningful connection with the past.

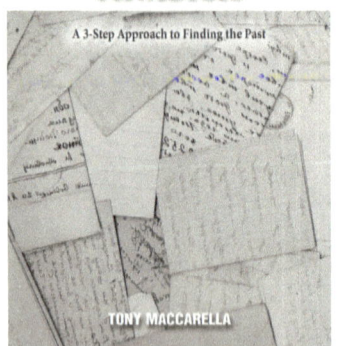

EFFECTIVE - Guided examples in each lesson give you a hands-on demonstration for every type of historical document.

ENGAGING - Tony's relaxed tone and engaging anecdotes make a daunting task less intimidating and never boring.

ESSENTIAL - Individual lessons directly address 20 different document types so you develop a complete foundation of this valuable skill.

MDA will give you the tools you need to think through any type of source, glean what matters, develop a contextual understanding, and assess the source as historical evidence. Grades 7-12. 120 p.

ISBN:	978-0-9905471-7-4 (print)	list: $18.00	bulk: $12.00
	978-1-948641-25-8 (ebook)	list: $10.00	bulk: $ 7.00

www.ingramcontent.com/pod-product-compliance
Lightning Source LLC
Chambersburg PA
CBHW030156100526
44592CB00009B/313